CALLED TOGETHER

Called Together has been an answer to prayer for us. We knew when we got married that God had called us to counsel other couples, but were searching for resources. These materials have been such an asset to both the engaged couples and our own marriage.

Gary and Gina Starr
Hillsborough, NJ

I have found this resource to be extremely beneficial in my work as I give oversight to the premarital preparation of couples here at our church. I have been anxiously awaiting the new release with all of its expanded information.

Bradley L. Hoopes
Associate Pastor, Congregational Bible Church

Spending time working through and discussing issues raised in this book was a wonderful way of preparing sensibly for our marriage, especially since we come from two countries which look at marriage in different ways. We consider *Called Together* essential for any couple preparing for marriage, all the more so if they come from different cultures.

Peter and RuthAnn Bunton
Directors of Holmsted Manor, Youth With a Mission
England

As a professional marriage counselor and pastor, I feel this biblically based resource is of great value in preparing engaged couples for a successful marriage. It encourages honesty and stimulates open communication.

Steve Lalor
Marriage Counselor and Pastor

The exercises in *Called Together* help couples reach inside themselves and talk about essential issues. And the postmarital sessions are a good way to see how the couple is doing in the most difficult period, the first year of marriage.

Andre Bustanoby
Author of *Being a Single Parent*

This premarital workbook effectively equipped us in the process of discovering each other. We came away with a better understanding of each other's hopes, fears and dreams for the future as well as our expectations of marriage.

Mel and Cindy Sensenig
Elizabethtown, PA

Called Together

*Asks the difficult questions
that all couples must answer
before and after they say "I do"*

Steve and Mary Prokopchak

HORIZON BOOKS

A DIVISION OF CHRISTIAN PUBLICATIONS, INC.
CAMP HILL, PENNSYLVANIA

HORIZON BOOKS

A Division of Christian Publications, Inc.
3825 Hartzdale Drive, Camp Hill, PA 17011
www.cpi-horizon.com
www.christianpublications.com

Called Together
ISBN: 0-88965-171-X
© 1999 by Horizon Books

00 01 02 03 04   6 5 4 3 2

This premarital training manual is dedicated first
to the Author of marriage, our Lord Jesus Christ,
and second to our children, Joshua, Marc and Brooke,
wonderful blessings from our call together.

Contents

Foreword xi

Preface xiii

Introduction xv

Congratulations! xvii

Preliminary Information xix

BEFORE YOU MARRY

Session One: About Me 1

Session Two: About Us 13

Session Three: Let's Talk 29

Session Four: Finances 43

Session Five: Sexual Relations 55

Session Six: Ceremony Planning 67

AFTER THE CEREMONY

Congratulations! 88

Session One: Three Months 89

Session Two: Nine Months 113

WHEN CHRISTIANS REMARRY

When Christians Remarry 137

INTERCULTURAL MARRIAGES

Intercultural Marriages 169

When Seniors Remarry

When Seniors Remarry 193

Appendices

Appendix A: Are You on Schedule? 207
Appendix B: Who Pays for What? 211
Appendix C: Birth Control 213
Appendix D: Honeymoon Precautions...217
Appendix E: Answer Key 219
Appendix F: Resource List..221

Counselor's Guide

Counselor's Guide...225

Foreword

With the myriad of marriages failing in America, every engaged couple needs to consider how to improve their odds of having a lifelong marriage. Fortunately, it is nearly possible to get "marriage insurance"—drastically improving the likelihood that their marriage will go the distance—if couples take several proven steps in advance of the wedding. What are those steps?

Based on my reporting in a nationally syndicated column, "Ethics and Religion," since 1981 and my work as president of an organization called Marriage Savers, I have come across the five most important steps a seriously dating or engaged couple can take to prepare for a great marriage. All of them may be seen in *Called Together*, written by the experienced mentoring couple, Steve and Mary Prokopchak:

1. Do not cohabit. According to the University of Wisconsin's *National Survey of Families and Households,* 40 out of 100 couples who cohabit separate before a wedding, and 45 of the 60 remaining will divorce, leaving only 15 out of 100 couples together after ten years.

2. Remain chaste. The sexually experienced have divorce rates two-thirds higher than those who are not, according to a key study.

3. Take a premarital inventory to get an objective view of strengths and weaknesses.

4. Be mentored by an older couple who can help engaged couples talk through issues that counseling brings up.

5. Use a workbook such as *Called Together* to learn biblical principles of how to build a lifelong marriage. This book that you hold in your hands can have a profound impact on you as a person, as a future husband or wife and as a parent. It will require a lot of quiet study of Scripture, an honest self-assessment of your communication and conflict resolution skills and a knowledge of yourself, your partner and your relationship that few couples acquire by simply dating.

Most young people look for the "perfect mate." But what the Prokopchaks are saying is that you must *be* the perfect mate. You must work on the many ways *you* can build a marriage on the solid rock of Christ. If you do so, and continue to invest energy and commitment, the Prokopchaks and I believe you will have an enduring marriage that brings glory to God and to your children and grandchildren.

Mike McManus
President, Marriage Savers

Preface

During 1970, my wife, LaVerne, and I had the privilege of ministering to hundreds of young people each week. It was a sheer joy witnessing the grace of God in these young lives. They were young radicals who had chosen to give their all to build the kingdom of God. Eventually, these young men and women began to establish meaningful relationships. The next step was marriage.

In 1980, we obeyed the Lord's call to pioneer a new church filled with many of these same young people. We tried our best to teach them practical biblical principles to properly prepare them for this massive step: two becoming one in "holy matrimony." In retrospect, the instruction that was being given to these young couples during those days was "weighed in the scales and found wanting."

Steve Prokopchak joined our ministry team in 1987 and began to develop a counseling ministry for this new church. I was impressed with Steve's ability to trust the Word of God and the Holy Spirit as he gave clear biblical and practical counseling. He spoke into people's lives with compassion. After four years of writing and re-writing, *Called Together* emerged. The results have been tremendous!

A practical, insightful and helpful book, *Called Together* has revolutionized premarital and postmarital counseling in our congregation. We have seen these scriptural principles worked out in the lives of the authors and in hundreds of engaged and married couples. With its clear biblical approach, *Called Together* helps engaged couples come face-to-face with real issues that they will confront throughout their lives together.

Requests for the *Called Together* materials have come from five continents of the world. Not only have these materials been used by pastors and counselors throughout North America, but materials have also been sent to Europe, Africa, Central America, South America, New Zealand and the Caribbean.

Thank you, Steve and Mary, for allowing the Lord to use you to help prepare engaged couples for marriage in a way that is scriptural and down-to-earth. May our Lord Jesus Christ be praised!

Larry and LaVerne Kreider
Senior Pastors
DOVE Christian Fellowship
Ephrata, Pennsylvania

Introduction

Traveling in many different countries of the world, we have discovered that few churches engage in adequate preparation and training for marriage. If marriage was introduced by the God that we know and love, shouldn't the Christian church take the mandate of "two becoming one" more seriously? Couples are spending 200 plus hours preparing for a one-day ceremony. And yet, this ceremony does nothing to build a couple's foundation for a lifetime together.

When we train pre- and postmarital counselors we often ask, "Did you receive premarital training?" The replies are frequently humorous. Some couples tell us they cannot remember. (What an impact their counseling had on them!) Others tell us "yes," but they cannot remember how many sessions were held. Even fewer couples can recall what was taught while attending premarital sessions with their pastor. One couple told us they had two sessions and then were forced to quit. When asked why, the couple said, "We were seeing a psychologist and could no longer afford to pay for the counseling."

When we, the authors, announced our engagement, the next item on the agenda was scheduling premarital counseling with our pastor. Our one and only session was held in the pastor's home with only the pastor. Our session lasted forty-five minutes and the only topic we can recall was that of submission.

As we look back, we realize that most churches were following the same format in the 1970s; our premarital counseling was average or even better than what some couples received—none.

In retrospect, we wish we could have had a mentoring couple to come alongside us, to share with us, pray with us, encourage us and hold us accountable in our relationship before and after the wedding day.

It is our desire to see couples trained to the honor and glory of God. We believe that the results of this training will validate our reasons for offering this course of study.

This manual is to be provocative by nature. It is designed to challenge you into wholehearted, Christ-centered commitment or to cause you to rethink your decision for marriage.

Called Together is best facilitated couple-to-couple, a counselor couple with a premarital couple. Michael McManus, in his book *Marriage Savers*, advocates the couple-to-couple mentoring approach when he states, "No one is better equipped to help . . . couples begin married life than a seasoned, mature couple with a solid marriage." He adds, "Mentor couples can be practical role models to other couples and give precious time that the pastor does not have. Such people are the greatest untapped resource for saving marriages."

We would like to present six reasons for premarital education: (1) maintaining a realistic perspective during the engagement period; (2) developing marital skills; (3) provoking serious thought concerning a lifelong commitment; (4) preventing problems in the future; (5) assessing the present relationship; (6) developing goals and long-term vision for the covenant relationship.

The home is the basic unit of the kingdom of God. As the home is established and restored, so will the kingdom of God be established and restored. We desire to see the kingdom of God established in every nation. This long-term vision will unfold as men and women of God, as families, are called together and then are called to go to the uttermost parts of the earth.

This course is for you if you are engaged to be married, if you are planning marriage someday or if you are newly married.

Congratulations!

Congratulations to the two of you in your desire to spend your lives together serving God.

We appreciate your willingness to be involved in premarital education. This course is designed to prepare you for God's call to marriage. These will be some of the most important counseling sessions you will ever be involved in. Marriage preparation counseling must be a time of thorough searching and communication concerning your past, your present and your dreams for the future.

In preparation for your first session, please carefully and prayerfully complete the following items: About Me, Spiritual Overview, Individual Mission, A Biblical Concept of Love, Sexual Boundaries and Who I Am in Christ. A Biblical Concept of Love is the only assignment you will work on together. You may complete the assignment Who I Am in Christ at your own pace.

Please take all of your assignments seriously, complete them thoroughly and turn them in to your counselors before each session. This will aid your counselors and help you complete the counseling process smoothly.

Even before this process is finished, you will see an improvement in the quality of your relationship. After you are married you will understand more fully the purpose of preparation for marriage by building a thorough foundation.

Expect a meaningful experience. Be prepared for loving, honest and challenging counselors. Do not hesitate to ask relevant questions of your fiancé and your counselors.

God bless you in your call together!

Preliminary Information

Counseling Schedule

Use this schedule to plan and to keep a record of your counseling appointments.

Session	Date	Time	Place
1			
2			
3			
4			
5			
6			
1			
2			

Identification Data

Name: _____

Address: _____

City: _____ State: _____ Zip Code: _____

Occupation: _____

Sex: _____ Birth Date: _____

Premarital Status: Single _____ Separated _____

Divorced _____ Widowed _____

Education (Circle last year completed)   High School 8 9 10 11 12

College 1 2 3 4 5 6 +

Church Affiliation _____

Health Information

Rate your physical health:

Very good _____ Good _____ Average _____ Declining _____ Other _____

Your approximate weight _____ lbs.

Recent weight changes: Lost _____ Gained _____

List important present or past illnesses: _____

_____

Date of last medical exam: _____

Your physician _____

Address: _____

Have you used drugs for other than medical purposes? Yes _____ No _____

Are you presently taking medication? Yes _____ No _____

Have you ever had a severe emotional upset? Yes _____ No _____

Have you ever had any psychotherapy or individual counseling?

     Yes _____ No _____

Have you ever had an abortion? Yes _____ No _____

Have you ever been involved in a relationship in which an abortion was per-
formed to terminate a pregnancy? Yes _____ No _____

Religious Background

Do you consider yourself a Christian? Yes _____ No _____

If yes, did you accept Christ as your Savior? Yes _____ No _____

Do you have a regular devotional time? Yes _____ No _____

Are you engaging in family or individual worship/devotions? Yes _____ No _____

Explain any recent changes or problems with your spiritual walk.

_____

_____

Personality

Have you ever suffered from depression? Yes _____ No _____

If yes, when? _____

Have you ever been involved in a cult, the occult, astrology, etc.?

     Yes _____ No _____

Explain _____

_____

Do you fear anything? (e.g., are you afraid of the dark, dying, the loss of a
parent, etc.?) _____

_____

Marriage Information
(If previously married)

How long did you know your former spouse before marriage? _____

Length of engagement _____

Is your previous spouse deceased?   Yes _____   No _____

Did you divorce?   Yes _____   No _____   When did this occur? _____

Did you receive premarital instruction?   Yes _____   No _____

Children:

Name _____ Age __ Sex __ Living with You? Yes __ No __

Name _____ Age __ Sex __ Living with You? Yes __ No __

Name _____ Age __ Sex __ Living with You? Yes __ No __

Parental History

Were you raised by your natural parents?   Yes _____   No _____

Are your parents still living?   Yes _____   No _____

What is (was) your parents' religious affiliation? (e.g., Methodist, Catholic, etc.)

_____

_____

Are (were) they Christians?   Yes _____   No _____

Are your parents still living together?   Yes _____   No _____

If your parents are separated or divorced, when did this occur? _____

Rate your parent's marriage: Happy _____   Average _____   Unhappy _____

As a child, did you feel closest to your: Father ___   Mother ___   Other ___

Was your childhood: Happy _____   Average _____   Unhappy _____

How many brothers and sisters do you have?   Brothers _____   Sisters _____

What number child were you in the birth order? _____

Other

Is there any other information you feel is important? _____

_____

_____

Important: Please elaborate on any area concerning premarital education that you would like to see covered. The following are some examples to help you identify specific areas of concern:

Different cultural backgrounds
Social activities
Future plans
Employment
Finances
Parents or future in-laws
Physical boundaries during engagement
Bad habits
Conflict in communication
Wedding plans

Other areas of concern:

_____

_____

Before You Marry

About Me

Premarital Session One

Taking an honest and intimate look at yourself and your partner is fundamental to the development and maintenance of unity within your marriage relationship. This session will challenge you to explore and understand yourself more fully.

When you and your partner come together in Session One with your premarital counselors, you will be given the opportunity to share about yourself and listen to your partner. Understanding one another will be a continuing process during your marriage relationship. Some of the most important foundational material will be discussed in this session. Speak truthfully and listen intently.

We encourage you to be honest as you answer the following questions and complete the open-ended statements. Allow this first session to be a meaningful experience for you and your fiancé.

About Me

Complete the following open-ended statements with what first comes to mind. Do this exercise separately.

1. I see myself as _____

2. A word that would best describe me is _____

3. Success in life to me is _____

4. My strongest quality is _____

5. One of my weaknesses is _____

6. Others view me as _____

7. I become quiet when _____

8. When others have a different opinion than I do, my reaction is to _____

9. My feelings tend to be hurt when _____

10. I feel guilty when _____

11. I worry when _____

12. I feel accepted when _____

13. What makes me feel inadequate is _____

14. I feel depressed when _____

_____

15. I receive pleasure from _____

_____

16. I am disappointed when _____

_____

17. Some of my gifts include _____

_____

18. My self-confidence falters when _____

_____

19. I get defensive when _____

_____

20. Something that makes me laugh is _____

_____

21. I get angry when _____

_____

22. When angry with someone, I tend to _____

_____

23. I receive great satisfaction from _____

_____

24. I feel trapped when _____

_____

25. I am afraid when _____

_____

Spiritual Overview

Complete the following statements concerning your spiritual life without the assistance of your fiancé.

1. My relationship with Jesus Christ is _____
   _____

2. My definition of *sin* is _____
   _____

3. Describe how you deal with sin. _____
   _____

4. Is Jesus Lord of your life? Please elaborate. _____
   _____

5. Have you been water baptized since accepting Christ? Yes ____ No ____
   If not, why not? Be prepared to share your experience. _____
   _____

6. As a believer, what is your experience with the Holy Spirit? ____
   _____

7. Describe your prayer life (where? when? why? etc.). _____
   _____

8. I read the Bible (when? for what reasons? etc.) _____
   _____

9. My personal commitment to attending a church (body of believers) is (how often? for what reasons? etc.) _____

_____

_____

10. My understanding of God is _____

_____

_____

11. In a spiritual sense, marriage will solve the following problems: _____

_____

_____

12. I would like to make the following change(s) in my own spiritual life:

_____

_____

_____

Individual Mission

Complete this assignment without the input of your fiancé. What you express will be your individual desire and call from God.

Jesus came to do the will of the Father who sent Him (John 6:38). God, as well, has a plan for your life. Read First Corinthians 12:12-20, 27, and write about what you see as God's mission for you. For example, you may believe God wants you to be a youth leader, Sunday school teacher, business owner, mother or foreign missionary.

_____

_____

_____

_____

_____

_____

_____

_____

_____

_____

_____

_____

_____

_____

_____

_____

_____

Biblical Concept of Love

The following Scripture references, along with a word study on the three types of love, will provide an overview of the basic ingredient in healthy family relationships. Take the necessary time to read and study this exercise with your fiancé.

Eros—A love that seeks its own. Unlike agape love, it is self-centered, sensual and inspired by selfish human nature. It is conditional love.

Phileo—A brotherly-friendship-companionship type of love. Phileo denotes mutual attraction, cooperation and communication between two individuals.

Agape—A self-giving love that does not seek anything in return. It's a love that endures even when another person becomes unlovable. It is like God's love, self-sacrificing and other-centered.

Scriptural study of love:

Matthew 22:37-39	Love God first
Luke 6:27-35	Love your enemies
John 13:34	Love one another
Romans 13:8-10	Love is the fulfillment of the law
1 Corinthians 8:1	Love edifies
Galatians 5:13	Serve through love
Galatians 6:2	Bear one another's burdens
Ephesians 4:2	Bear with one another in love
Ephesians 5:25	Husbands, love as Christ loved
1 Peter 4:8	Love covers sins
1 John 3:16-18	Love is laying down your life
1 Corinthians 13	The most excellent way

Sexual Boundaries

As the process of premarital counseling begins, it is important to consider your sexual boundaries. Many couples express that they will not be involved in sexual intercourse, but have not taken the time to communicate beyond this point. The following exercise, to be completed individually, will challenge you to know where your sexual boundaries are. Consequently, you will know when you are approaching the limit you have set for yourself and your fiancé.

Below is an example of physical progression of intimacy in a relationship:

1. Holding hands
2. Arm around shoulder/waist
3. Embracing
4. Kissing on the cheek
5. Kissing on the lips
6. French kissing
7. Fondling sexual areas
8. Sexual intercourse

Take time to write your responses to the following questions.

1. As an engaged couple, have you discussed your physical boundaries?

   Yes _____ No _____

   Write about physical boundaries as you and your fiancé interpret them.

   _____

   _____

2. Have you moved beyond these boundaries in your relationship?

   Yes _____ No _____

3. Are you currently living together or have you been involved in cohabitation in the past?

   _____

   _____

4. My definition of fornication is . . . _____

_____

5. Discuss the negative impact fornication may have on your relationship.

_____

_____

6. Are there places that should be "off limits" for you as a couple?

_____

7. Are there times you and your fiancé should not be alone together?

_____

8. First Thessalonians 4:1-8 states God's will for you concerning sexual
   areas. What is His will? _____

_____

9. Read Ephesians 5:3-11. How does this Scripture relate to sexual
   boundaries? _____

_____

10. How can you relate First Timothy 5:1-2 to your relationship with your
    fiancé? _____

_____

11. List the specific steps you can take to prevent sexual impurity.

_____

_____

12. Developing a key word or phrase to speak to one another that indicates
    you are approaching your physical boundaries would be helpful. Prepare
    for your next premarital session by jotting down some possible key
    words or phrases. _____

_____

Now that you have completed this exercise, make a commitment to communicate
with your fiancé and your premarital counselors about your personal boundaries. Ask
your counselors to help hold you as a couple accountable in the sexual area.

Who I Am in Christ

First Thessalonians 5:23 states that we are spirit, soul and body. Normally, we feed the body three meals a day. The soul is educated and fed emotionally. This exercise is designed to nourish the spirit, that part of us in which God dwells. Study the following Scriptures together and individually to discover who you are in Christ.

I am now God's child . . . . 1 John 3:2
I am born of the incorruptible seed of God's Word . . . . 1 Peter 1:23
I am loved by Christ . . . . Revelation 1:5
I am forgiven of all my sins . . . . Ephesians 1:7
I am justified from all things . . . . Acts 13:39
I am the righteousness of God . . . . 2 Corinthians 5:21
I am free from all condemnation . . . . Romans 8:1
I can forget the past . . . . Philippians 3:13
I am a new creature . . . . 2 Corinthians 5:17
I am the temple of the Holy Spirit . . . . 1 Corinthians 6:19
I am redeemed from the curse of the law . . . . Galatians 3:13
I am accepted in Christ . . . . Ephesians 1:6
I am reconciled to God . . . . 2 Corinthians 5:18
I am beloved of God . . . . 1 John 4:10
I am a saint . . . . Romans 1:7
I am holy and without blame before Him . . . . Ephesians 1:4
I am the head and not the tail . . . . Deuteronomy 28:13
I am called of God . . . . 2 Timothy 1:9
I am brought near by the blood of Christ . . . . Ephesians 2:13
I am complete in Christ . . . . Colossians 2:10
I am delivered from the power of darkness . . . . Colossians 1:13
I am an ambassador for Christ . . . . 2 Corinthians 5:20
I am the salt of the earth . . . . Matthew 5:13
I am the light of the world . . . . Matthew 5:14
I am dead to sin . . . . Romans 6:2
I am alive to God . . . . Romans 6:11
I am raised up with Christ and seated in heavenly realms . . . Ephesians 2:6

I am a king and a priest to God. . . . . Revelation 1:6
I am loved with an everlasting love . . . . Jeremiah 31:3
I am fit to partake of His inheritance. . . . . Colossians 1:12
I am an heir of God and a joint heir with Christ . . . . Romans 8:17
I am more than a conqueror. . . . . Romans 8:37
I am healed by the wounds of Jesus. . . . . 1 Peter 2:24
I am built on the foundation of the apostles and prophets,
    with Jesus Christ Himself as the chief cornerstone. . . . . Ephesians 2:20
I am in Christ Jesus by God's act . . . . 1 Corinthians 1:30
I am kept by God's power . . . . 1 Peter 1:5
I am sealed with the promised Holy Spirit . . . . Ephesians 1:13
I have everlasting life . . . . John 5:24
I am crucified with Christ . . . . Galatians 2:20
I am a partaker of the divine nature . . . . 2 Peter 1:4
I have been given all things that pertain to life. . . . . 2 Peter 1:3
I have been blessed with every spiritual blessing . . . . Ephesians 1:3
I have peace with God . . . . Romans 5:1
I proclaim God's praise . . . . 1 Peter 2:9
I can do all things through Christ. . . . . Philippians 4:13
I have all my needs met by God according to His
    riches in glory in Christ Jesus . . . . Philippians 4:19
I shall do even greater works than Christ Jesus . . . . John 14:12
I am being kept strong to the end . . . . 1 Corinthians 1:8
I am chosen. . . . . 1 Thessalonians 1:4
I overcome the world . . . . 1 John 5:4
I have a guaranteed inheritance . . . . Ephesians 1:14
I am a fellow citizen with the saints . . . . Ephesians 2:19
I am free . . . . John 8:36
I always triumph in Christ . . . . 2 Corinthians 2:14
I am in Jesus Christ's hands . . . . John 10:28
I am holy, without blemish and free from accusation . . . . Colossians 1:22
Christ in me is the hope of glory . . . . Colossians 1:27

About Us

Premarital Session Two

Many couples enter marriage unrealistically. God wants us to be full of faith but "wise as serpents." With the great wealth of literature, videos and tapes available to us on the subjects of marriage, sex, finances, communication and so forth, no couple should enter marriage unaware of Satan's devices to undermine and destroy relationships.

Why do you want to marry this particular person? How do you and your fiancé know that God is calling you together? What are your expectations for this marriage? How would you react to potentially difficult circumstances should they arise during your marriage? Are your parents in agreement with your engagement? Assignments for Session Two address these questions. This session will also help you to assess your expectations and perceptions of marriage and will end with the two of you working on a cooperative mission. Please be aware that you will need to copy pages 22 and 23, "Parent Questionnaire," for your parents to complete and turn into your premarital counselors with other chapter two homework.

God has a perfect design for marriage. When conflicts or difficult circumstances arise, God's Word offers help and hope for each situation.

Reasons for Marriage

Answer the following questions without the help of your fiancé.

1. In your own words, define marriage. _____

    _____

    _____

    _____

    _____

2. Have you thought through your reasons for marrying your fiancé? List ten of those reasons.

    1. _____

    _____

    _____

    2. _____

    _____

    _____

    3. _____

    _____

    _____

    4. _____

    _____

    _____

    5. _____

    _____

    _____

    6. _____

    _____

    _____

    7. _____

    _____

8. _____
   _____
   _____

9. _____
   _____
   _____

10. _____
    _____
    _____

3. What confirmation do you and your fiancé have that God is calling you together? Please elaborate. _____
   _____
   _____
   _____

4. Why is this the right time in your life to marry? _____
   _____
   _____
   _____

5. Marriage is for the mature. List some characteristics and evidences of maturity that you see in yourself and your fiancé. _____
   _____
   _____
   _____
   _____
   _____
   _____
   _____
   _____

Expectations and Perceptions of Marriage

A. Without the help of your fiancé, list ten expectations you will have of your fiancé when you are married. For example, a husband might expect his wife never to be employed outside the home, to balance the checkbook, to mow the lawn or to perform all household duties. A wife might expect her husband to be the head of the family, to administer all child discipline, to help with housework or to decrease sports activities with his friends.

1. _____

2. _____

3. _____

4. _____

5. _____

6. _____

7. _____

8. _____

9. _____

10. _____

B. Without the help of your fiancé, consider your expectations in the area of household chores. Below is a list of chores. Who will be responsible for the completion of these chores? Mark *H* for husband, *W* for wife or *S* for shared.

Washing dishes   _____

Laundry   _____

Ironing   _____

Cleaning vehicles   _____

Washing windows   _____

Cleaning bathrooms   _____

Meal preparation   _____

Pet care   _____

Collecting trash   _____

Mowing the lawn   _____

Gardening   _____

Dusting   _____

Vacuuming   _____

Making the bed   _____

Grocery shopping   _____

Vehicle maintenance   _____

When meeting with your premarital counselors, take the time to discuss any differences you discover regarding chore and household expectations.

The following are some tips for you and your fiancé to keep in mind:
- Make chores a team effort.
- Decide which chores each person is responsible for.
- Share less desirable chores.
- If there is a chore that you desire to be completed a certain way, then you should do that task.
- Keep in mind, chores do not have to be equally divided.

Reactions

How would you react to the following circumstances?

1. You and your spouse are scheduled to work opposite shifts. _____
_____
_____

2. You discover that your spouse deals with jealousy. _____
_____
_____

3. Your spouse no longer has time for daily devotions. _____
_____
_____

4. A friend becomes flirtatious with your spouse. _____
_____
_____

5. You cannot get along with your sister-in-law. _____
_____
_____

6. You have a communication problem with your mother-in-law. _____
_____
_____

7. You have difficulty becoming pregnant. _____
_____
_____

8. Your apartment is too small and you cannot afford a larger one. _____
_____
_____

9. Your spouse spends more money on himself/herself than on you. _____

_____

_____

10. You discover your spouse has incurred significant credit card debt.

_____

_____

11. Your spouse is laid off from his/her job. _____

_____

_____

12. Your sex life is less than exciting. _____

_____

_____

13. Communication becomes increasingly difficult. _____

_____

_____

14. You discover that your spouse cannot let go of his/her mother. _____

_____

_____

15. A job change requires you and your spouse to move to the other side of the country. _____

_____

_____

16. You find yourself battling attraction to a coworker. _____

_____

_____

Our Parents

Families of origin play a vital role when two persons are considering a lifetime together. Discuss your feelings about your parents and your future in-laws by answering the following questions.

1. Have you communicated to your parents your desire to be married?
   Yes _____ No _____

2. Are your father and mother in agreement with your plans for marriage?
   Yes _____ No _____

3. Do your parents agree with the length of your engagement and the date of the wedding? Yes _____ No _____

4. Have your parents expressed any hesitations concerning your desire to be married? Yes _____ No _____

5. Have your parents met your fiancé's parents? Yes _____ No _____

6. Do you feel your parents are supportive of the person you want to marry?
   Yes _____ No _____

7. Are your parents Christians? Yes _____ No _____
   If not, how will that affect your relationship now or after you are married?

   _____

   _____

8. Will you attend your parents' church? Yes _____ No _____

9. Have you asked your parents for any wisdom or advice that they may have for you? Yes _____ No _____ If so, what advice have they shared with you? _____

   _____

10. How can you maintain a spirit of honor toward your parents after you are married? _____

   _____

11. How often do you plan to visit your parents after you are married?

_____

_____

12. How will you respond to advice from your parents that you don't agree with? _____

_____

13. Are there other matters concerning your parents or your fiancé's parents that you have questions about? _____

_____

14. I would like my marriage to be like my parents' marriage in the following ways: _____

_____

_____

_____

_____

_____

15. I desire my marriage to differ from my parents' marriage in these ways:

_____

_____

_____

_____

_____

_____

_____

Parent Questionnaire

We believe it is important to include parents as we help couples prepare for marriage. You have invested much love, time, energy and finances into raising and training your child in order to see him/her come to this point in his/her life. Please respond in writing to the following questions and return them to your son or daughter so that they may be shared in their next premarital counseling session.

1. Describe your relationship with your son or daughter . . . _____

    _____

    _____

    future son-in-law or daughter-in-law . . . _____

    _____

    _____

2. Express how you will help your child leave you and cleave to his/her spouse.

    _____

    _____

    _____

3. Are you aware of any reasons that would prohibit this couple from marrying at this time? _____

    _____

    _____

4. How often do you expect to have visits with the newly married couple?

    _____

    _____

    _____

5. An area of adjustment that we foresee in our son's or daughter's marriage could be . . . _____

_____

_____

6. Are you able to express a written word of blessing to this marriage? If yes, please expound below. If no, why not? Please explain. _____

_____

_____

_____

_____

_____

_____

_____

_____

_____

(Permission is granted to photocopy this assignment only. One copy may be made for each parent.)

"A Letter to My Parents"

As a way to honor your parents (Ephesians 6:2-3), on a separate sheet of paper compose a short letter of appreciation to them. Below are areas that you may consider reflecting upon.

- Life
- Spiritual heritage
- Financial values
- Moral guidance
- Physical provision
- Encouragement
- Emotional support
- Education
- Athletic encouragement
- Discipline/training
- Love/affirmation/acceptance/approval
- Work ethic/skills
- Sacrifices/commitment

Please make a copy of this letter for yourself.

Are You Ready to Leave and Cleave?

Marriage predates Christianity. It goes back to Genesis, chapter 1. This study gives you and your fiancé the opportunity to discover God's design for marriage. Review the Scriptures together and then with your premarital counselors.

1. Genesis 1:26-27

The place to start. . . . In the beginning, God had a specific design in mind when He created man and instituted marriage. We were designed in His image, His likeness. He gave us dominion over the animals of the earth. God created both male and female.

2. Genesis 2:7, 21-22

Man was made from the dust of the earth, and God breathed the breath of life into him. Woman was created from the man. She was specifically designed to correspond to the man. Eve was "fashioned," while Adam was "formed."

3. Genesis 2:18

Man's first need from God was a "helper suitable for him." God met the first problem man encountered—loneliness. As Adam named the animals, he noticed that none of them were even close to being "suitable" or of his kind.

4. Genesis 2:23 and Ephesians 5:31

Eve was given to Adam by God, and Adam said, "This is now bone of my bones and flesh of my flesh; she shall be called 'woman', for she was taken out of man." Eve was physically, spiritually, intellectually, emotionally and relationally suitable for Adam. She was not like the animals. She was of the same flesh. A part of Adam's structure was used to fashion Eve.

Man's strength is more external while woman's strength is internal. A man desires to be noticed for what he accomplishes. A woman wants to be valued for who she is as a person. For Adam to be Adam, he needed Eve.

5. Genesis 2:24; Matthew 19:4-5 and Mark 10:6-8

Before joining and cleaving, there needs to be a leaving. We leave father and mother to establish a new family unit. The focus becomes one another. Former friends, jobs and extended family take on a lesser priority than this new union. This new household is under new authority. One man walks the bride up the wedding aisle (the father). Then another man (the new husband) walks her back the aisle. Dr. Ed Wheat said, "Don't leave unless you plan to cleave."

6. Genesis 2:24 and Ephesians 5:31-32

Marriage means that two persons become one. John is Sue and Sue is John. What affects John affects Sue. These two persons are now united. This union must be heterosexual and monogamous (see Proverbs 5:15-23; 6:23-33).

There are three expressions of oneness in Scripture. These three expressions are (1) the trinity (2 Corinthians 13:14); (2) Christ and the church (Ephesians 5:25-27, 31-32); and (3) marriage (Genesis 2:24, Ephesians 5:31).

The number one cannot be divided without the result being two halves. Separation and/or divorce is a separation of one person. This separation leaves two fractions of one.

Cooperative Mission

In Session One, you wrote about your individual mission or call from God. Genesis 1:28-30 and Genesis 2:15 reveal that Adam and Eve received instruction from God to be involved in a cooperative mission. God gave the garden, the earth and the animals to Adam and Eve to care for together. When two become one, it is important not only to know our individual mission but also to understand our cooperative mission from the Lord. Take a moment with your fiancé to write about how you see yourself involved after marriage in a cooperative mission with your future spouse. (For example: Brian is a vital part of the church worship team, and Megan teaches a Sunday school class for preschoolers. Those are individual missions. Together, Brian and Megan lead a home group for junior highers. That is a cooperative mission.)

_____

_____

_____

_____

_____

_____

_____

_____

_____

_____

_____

_____

_____

_____

_____

Let's Talk

Premarital Session Three

An effective communication system is vital to a stable, intimate and satisfying marriage relationship. A breakdown of communication is almost always a primary cause of marital dysfunction. Ed Cole, author of *Communication, Sex, and Money*, states that when communication stops, abnormality sets in, and the ultimate end of abnormality is death of the relationship. Just as faith dies when we refuse to communicate with our heavenly Father, so will a marriage die when a couple refuses to communicate. Ephesians 4:29-30 reveals that communication should edify, not corrupt. The Holy Spirit is grieved when we are not ministers of grace.

Our communication goals are to share with one another freely; to be lovingly honest about what we think and feel; to understand each other; to listen respectfully and respond appropriately; to be able to disagree and discuss our disagreements without becoming hurt or attacking one another; to have conversation that is beneficial and uplifting. We will work toward these communication goals through various homework assignments, including nonverbal communication, communication guidelines, effective communication and scenario communication.

Norm Wright, a well-known marriage counselor, states in his book *Training Christians to Counsel* that communication can be broken down as follows:

7% words (content)
38% attitude (tone of voice)
55% body language

Take this opportunity to begin to analyze your personal communication tendencies. What body language do you display when you are angry, hurt or selfish? Under what circumstances does your tone of voice change? Even if you feel communication is one of your strong points, give full attention to the assignments which follow. Scripture has a lot to say about the way we talk to each other. Be open to discovering some hindrances to good communication in your life.

Nonverbal Communication

1. List at least five ways in which you have experienced nonverbal communication from your fiancé (both positive and negative).

    1. _____
    2. _____
    3. _____
    4. _____
    5. _____

2. Share some experiences you have had concerning attitude and tone of voice while communicating with your fiancé. (Again, share at least one positive and one negative experience.)

    1. _____
    2. _____

3. Identify any factors that have hindered communication for you and your fiancé (for example: in-laws, past relationships, beliefs, etc.).

    1. _____
    2. _____
    3. _____
    4. _____
    5. _____

4. Study the following verses and record what they reveal to you concerning nonverbal communication.

    Genesis 3:7-10 _____
    _____
    _____

Genesis 4:5-6 _____

_____

_____

Genesis 40:6-7 _____

_____

_____

Joshua 7:6 _____

_____

_____

1 Samuel 18:3-4 _____

_____

_____

1 Kings 19:3-4 _____

_____

_____

1 Kings 21:4 _____

_____

_____

Proverbs 31:12-27 _____

_____

_____

Mark 2:3-5 _____

_____

_____

Luke 18:10-13 _____

_____

_____

1 John 3:17-18 _____

_____

_____

How Do We Talk Together?

What kind of interaction do you and your fiancé have with each other? Respond to the statements below by placing a check under the answer that best describes you and your fiancé.

	Always	Usually	Sometimes	Rarely	Never
1. I listen to my fiancé.					
2. My fiancé listens to me.					
3. I understand what my fiancé is trying to say.					
4. My fiancé understands what I am trying to say.					
5. I show appreciation when my fiancé does things for me.					
6. My fiancé shows appreciation when I do things for him/her.					
7. I show interest in my fiancé's ideas, thoughts, feelings and activities.					
8. My fiancé shows interest in my ideas, thoughts, feelings and activities.					
9. I feel comfortable disagreeing with what my fiancé says.					
10. I feel comfortable when my fiancé disagrees with me.					
11. I show interest in facts and information.					
12. My fiancé shows interest in facts and information.					
13. I am able to express feelings and emotions.					
14. My fiancé is able to express feelings and emotions.					
15. I am happy just to share and spend time with my fiancé.					

Communication Guidelines

Think about the following guidelines and study the supporting Scriptures. You may complete this assignment individually or together.

Part A:

1. Be a ready listener, and do not answer until the other person has finished talking (Proverbs 18:13; James 1:19).

2. Be slow to speak. Think first. Don't be hasty in your words. Speak in such a way that the other person can understand and accept what you say (Proverbs 15:23; 18:2; 29:20).

3. Don't go to bed angry! Each day, clear the offenses of that day. Speak the truth, but do it in love. Do not exaggerate (Ephesians 4:15, 25-26).

4. Do not use silence to frustrate the other person. Explain why you are hesitant to talk at this time (Proverbs 15:28; 16:23).

5. Do not become involved in heated disputes. It is possible to disagree without attacking (Proverbs 17:14; 20:3; Ephesians 4:31).

6. Do not respond in uncontrolled anger. Use a kind response and a soft tone voice (Proverbs 14:29; 15:1; 25:15; 29:11).

7. When you are wrong, admit it, ask for forgiveness and then ask how you can change (Proverbs 12:15; 16:2; 21:2; Matthew 5:23-25).

8. When someone confesses a wrong to you, tell that person you forgive him/her. Be sure it is forgiven and not brought up again to that person, to others or to yourself (Luke 17:3-4; Ephesians 4:32; Colossians 3:13).

9. Avoid nagging (Proverbs 10:19; 21:19; 27:15).

10. Do not blame or criticize the other person. Instead, restore, encourage and edify (Romans 14:13; Galatians 6:1; 1 Thessalonians 5:11).

11. If someone verbally attacks, criticizes or blames you, do not respond in the same manner (Romans 12:17, 21; 1 Peter 2:23; 3:9).

12. Try to understand the other person's opinions. Make allowances for differences (Ephesians 4:2; 1 Peter 2:23; 3:9).

13. Be concerned about the other person's interests (Philippians 2:4).

14. Do not gossip (Proverbs 17:9; 18:8; 20:19; 26:22).

Part B:

1. What attitudes or messages do the following sentences convey to you? Do they convey respect, appreciation, consideration, encouragement, affection and love—or disdain, disrespect, rudeness, animosity, hostility and rejection? Try to imagine someone saying these sentences to you.

"You don't really care." _____

_____

"I really need you." _____

_____

"Well, what do you have to complain about today?" _____

_____

"It sounds like you had a difficult day. Is there any way I can help you?"

_____

_____

"You shouldn't feel that way!" _____

_____

"I'm really sorry that you feel that way. How can I help? I'll be glad to pray for you and do anything I can." _____

_____

"You never kiss me." _____

_____

"Do you know what, honey? I really love you and like to have you hold me and kiss me." _____

_____

"Well, what do you know? Miracles still happen. You're ready on time."

_____

_____

"Hey, hon, I just wanted you to know that I really appreciated the way you hurried to be ready to go on time." _____

_____

"Honey, you're terrific, and getting better all the time." _____

_____

"You always forget what I ask you to do." _____

_____

"I like the way you smile. It really brightens my day." _____

_____

"We ought to have company more often. It's the only time we get good food around here." _____

_____

"That was a super meal. You're a fantastic cook." _____

_____

"How come you could get home early tonight when you don't do it other nights?"

_____

"Boy, it's really great you got home early. I miss you during the day."

_____

_____

"I can't believe there's no money in the checking account. What did you spend it on?" _____

_____

"Maybe there's a better way to discuss financial matters. Could we get some help?" _____

_____

Adapted from *A Homework Manual for Biblical Counseling, Volume 1* by Wayne Mack. Copyright 1979. Used by permission of Presbyterian and Reformed Publishing Company, Phillipsburg, New Jersey.

How to Become an Effective Communicator

Part A. The following Scriptures discuss interferences to healthy communication. As you study them individually, record the interferences in the blank provided. Number one has been completed as an example.

1. Ephesians 4:25   _Stop lying and speak the truth._
2. Ephesians 4:29 _____
3. Ephesians 4:31 _____
4. Colossians 3:8 _____
5. Colossians 3:9 _____
6. James 1:19 _____
7. Proverbs 11:13 _____
8. Proverbs 12:16 _____
9. Proverbs 12:18 _____
10. Proverbs 15:1 _____
11. Proverbs 15:5 _____
12. Proverbs 17:9 _____
13. Proverbs 18:2 _____
14. Proverbs 18:8 _____
15. Proverbs 18:13 _____
16. Proverbs 19:1 _____
17. Proverbs 19:5 _____
18. Proverbs 20:19 _____
19. Proverbs 25:24 _____
20. Proverbs 26:18-19 _____
21. Proverbs 26:20-21 _____
22. Proverbs 29:20 _____
23. Matthew 5:23-24 _____

Part B. From the previous list of Scriptures, what unhealthy patterns of communication can you identify in your own life?

1. _____

2. _____

3. _____

4. _____

5. _____

6. _____

7. _____

8. _____

9. _____

10. _____

Do You Discuss . . . ?

Do you and your fiancé discuss . . .

	Yes	No	Desire to
1. your feelings and attitudes?			
2. your differences?			
3. your hurts?			
4. plans that involve both of you?			
5. one another's faults?			
6. one another's families?			
7. your criticisms of one another?			
8. things you have noticed concerning your relationship but are afraid to talk about?			
9. jealousy you may have of one another?			
10. disagreements without losing your temper?			
11. how you will manage your money?			
12. your expectations of one another in parenting?			
13. your views on training children?			
14. matters when one of you is quiet or sulking?			
15. traditional versus nontraditional roles?			

Scenario Communication

Please indicate how you will respond to the following situations.

1. You have just arrived home from work. You are recounting an important conversation with your boss. Right in the middle of it your spouse asks, "Did you bring in the mail?" _____

_____

2. You are mowing the yard. Your spouse asks you to go to the store for some milk, but you really want to finish mowing. _____

_____

3. It has been over a week since the clothes were washed. You are out of socks.

_____

_____

4. You have had another heated discussion about your finances. Your spouse has purchased a non-budgeted item again. _____

_____

5. You notice that whenever you have something important or confrontational to discuss with your spouse, he or she yawns and seems disinterested.

_____

_____

6. It seems that your spouse has difficulty picking up and putting away his or her things. You're wondering if he or she notices the items left on the floor. _____

_____

_____

Praying Together

Couple prayer is the most vital ingredient to a committed, Christian marriage. The most intimate thing a couple can do together is to pray. Prayer is far more intimate than sex. When we pray with our mate, we discover their heart; we discover their most intimate needs and desires.

Mary and I have always prayed together throughout our marriage. However, it wasn't until our sons entered public high school that we became desperately serious about petitioning the Father together on a daily basis. We realized that providing a prayer covering for our children was the most important thing we could do for them.

Because prayer is so intimate, couples who are engaged should limit their prayer time as well as be conscious about where they pray together. Praying in a dark room or sitting on a couch could lead to sensual closeness. We believe that the enemy, making your most spiritual times together a temptation to be sensual, can confuse spirituality and sensuality. Be conscious of this fact.

Agreeing together in prayer (Amos 3:3; Matthew 18:19) is far more powerful than arguing together. Listen to Art Hunt's words in his book, *Praying with the One You Love* (Multnomah, 1996, page 29): "Praying with your spouse is perhaps the most intimate thing you can do together. Think of what happens when you pray. There you are, right in front of God—and He can see right through you! And there by your side is your partner. You are both literally 'unveiled' before God. You may have already said, 'I trust you' to your spouse, but this—mutual prayer—is where the real risk comes into play. . . . The bigger the risk, the bigger the reward. And in this case, the reward is enormous!"

Some couples do not pray together because of vulnerability (it's risking too much); others avoid prayer because of feeling inadequate; some use the excuse that they do not have enough time; others simply do not trust their spouse enough. Whatever the reason, all of these responses keep us from obedience to God, from growing together spiritually, from becoming passionately intimate and from agreement that brings the deepest unity any two persons can encounter.

Perhaps you've already begun praying together. If not, we encourage you to begin now. If you establish this life-giving habit now, it will flow into your marriage relationship quite naturally.

Work through the following exercise together:

1. When is the best time for us to pray together? _____
   _____
   _____

2. Are there places that we should avoid when praying together?
   _____
   _____

3. How can prayer lead to sensuality? _____
   _____
   _____

4. Before marriage, how much time should we spend praying together?
   _____
   _____

5. After marriage, our goal for prayer would be (how frequent and how
   long) . . . _____
   _____

6. Areas to cover in prayer before marriage might include: _____
   _____
   _____

7. Areas to cover in prayer after marriage can extend and also include:
   _____
   _____

Finances

Premarital Session Four

Agreement is basic in successful marriages. "Do two walk together unless they have agreed to do so?" (Amos 3:3). Financial agreement is an important marital goal. When partners agree on getting out of debt, tithing, overcoming a financial crisis or being better stewards, then the power of God is released to work in their lives.

God's Word offers clear guidelines and principles for handling money. A scriptural overview of finances is included in this session. You will also have opportunity to express your personal financial views, to describe your financial background, to complete a cost estimation exercise and to work on a budget profile.

God wants you to have a strategy for financial health. Discover a place of agreement and you will discover a place of blessing and provision.

Personal Financial Views

In order to discover and provide clarification on your personal financial views, answer the following questions without the help of your fiancé.

1. Will you have joint or separate checking accounts?   Joint _____ Separate _____

2. Who will do the bookkeeping? _____

3. Who will write the checks when paying bills? _____

4. Will you buy or rent a home?   Buy _____ Rent _____

    If renting, how soon do you expect to buy? _____

5. How often will you go out to dinner? _____

6. Will you maintain a monthly budget? Yes _____ No _____

7. Will you use credit cards or borrow money?   Yes _____ No _____

8. Will you buy a car with borrowed money?   Yes _____ No _____

9. What percentage of your paycheck should be saved each month? _____

10. Will you give tithes and offerings?   Yes _____ No _____

11. Will the wife return to work after having children?   Yes _____ No _____

12. What insurance(s) will you purchase? _____

13. Who will be responsible to make out a will? _____

14. How much freedom would you like to have when purchasing items without your spouse's approval? _____

15. How much spending money will you and your spouse normally have in your possession? _____

Financial Background

Given the assumption that your parents' views toward money will have a profound effect on your views, discuss what you have observed about your parents' finances. Be prepared to share how your views are similar to or different from your parents' views of money.

1. Did your parents maintain a budget?   Yes _____ No _____

2. Who was in charge of the finances? _____

3. Were the bills paid on time?   Yes _____ No _____

4. Were your parents generous with those in need? Yes _____ No _____

5. Did your parents agree or did they argue a lot concerning money?

   _____

6. Did they focus on the necessities or did they purchase a lot of luxuries?

   _____

7. Did they take family vacations? Yes _____ No _____

8. Did one or both parents have a spending allowance? _____

9. Did your parents place importance on saving their money?
   Yes _____ No _____

10. Did your parents tithe or support mission work?   Yes _____ No _____

11. How often did your family go out to eat? _____

12. How have your personal financial values been influenced by the financial values held by your parents? _____

   _____

Cost Estimation

Do you have any idea of the cost of the items you'll need to maintain your household or your own physical well-being (for example, food, clothes, tools for lawn care and household repairs)? Have fun and see how closely, without the help of your fiancé, you can estimate the cost of the following items.

1. A five-pound ham _____
2. A pound of American cheese _____
3. A pound of ground turkey _____
4. A can of cherry pie filling _____
5. A five-pound bag of sugar _____
6. A man's sport coat _____
7. A woman's swimsuit _____
8. A pair of pantyhose _____
9. A skirt and blouse _____
10. A nylon slip _____
11. A bottle of fingernail polish _____
12. A pair of women's shoes _____
13. A pair of men's slacks _____
14. A leather briefcase _____
15. A leather handbag _____
16. A haircut _____
17. A hair permanent _____

18. A tune-up for a V-6 engine _____
19. A case of motor oil _____
20. Front disc brakes _____
21. 100 pounds of lawn food _____
22. A six-foot wooden stepladder _____
23. A 22-inch lawn mower _____
24. A gallon of latex paint _____
25. Queen-size no-iron sheets _____
26. Two pairs of window curtains _____
27. A set of bath towels _____
28. A newspaper subscription _____
29. A child's baseball mitt _____
30. A deer hunting rifle _____
31. Two tickets to a football game _____
32. Two tickets to a play _____
33. A fishing license _____
34. A round of golf _____

Scriptural Truths about Finances

A. Read the following Scriptures with your fiancé and paraphrase the principles you derive from each passage.

1. Deuteronomy 8:17-18 _____

_____

2. Proverbs 11:24-25 _____

_____

3. Proverbs 11:28 _____

_____

4. Proverbs 13:22 _____

_____

5. Proverbs 22:1, 4, 7 _____

_____

6. Ecclesiastes 5:10 _____

_____

7. Jeremiah 9:23-24 _____

_____

8. Matthew 6:19-21 _____

_____

9. Luke 12:13-21 _____

_____

10. Romans 13:6-8 _____

_____

11. 1 Timothy 6:3-10, 17-18 _____

_____

12. Hebrews 13:5 _____

_____

B. Of the scriptural truths about finances listed on page 47, share any areas of specific concern to you personally or areas you believe need to be addressed with your fiancé.

_____

_____

_____

_____

_____

_____

_____

_____

_____

_____

_____

_____

_____

_____

_____

_____

_____

_____

_____

The Personal Finances Budget Sheet

When two people come together in marriage, an entirely new financial picture is created; two incomes merge into one. This presents potential conflict if the couple does not follow practical guidelines for managing money.

As you and your fiancé plan your proposed budget, use this budget sheet as a blueprint for your money management. Listing your assets and liabilities is good record keeping, and it will enable you and your counselors to "see" your spending plan, which in turn will help you to effectively control your expenditures. Use the finished product to establish financial goals and to set priorities.

Instructions

Along with your fiancé, record the known or estimated monthly dollar figure for each category on the budget sheet. (We've included two blank sheets for you.) The definitions of the categories are listed below to help you determine the scope of each one. The completed example on page 51 will serve as a guideline.

Tithe: List your regular support (tithe) to your church (anything over 10% may be listed under the *Giving* category).

Tax: List federal, state and county taxes.

Investment: List any money invested for future care of your family (IRAs, retirement programs, home savings, etc.).

Mortgage/Rent: List mortgage payment or rent payment.

Housing Maintenance: If you own your home, estimate monthly maintenance costs.

Utilities: List your monthly utility costs.

Telephone: Estimate your monthly phone bill.

Food & Supplies: Include food (work and school lunches), drugstore supplies, department store sundries (toiletries, laundry).

Clothing: Estimate a monthly budget.

Autos: List auto payment(s) and the cost of insurance, driver's licenses, vehicle registration, gas and maintenance.

Medical/Dental: Include health insurance payments and money spent for medicines, medical/dental/optical checkups.

Gifts: List monthly expenses for gifts (birthday, wedding, etc.).

Stationery: Estimate the cost of postage and stationery.

Dining: List restaurant meals.

Travel/Vacation: List weekend travel and yearly vacation.

Recreation/Entertainment: List money spent for family activities and sporting events (swimming, bowling, movies, football games, etc.).

Miscellaneous: List expenses not covered above (college loans, marriage seminars, periodical subscriptions, life insurance and personal debt).

Giving: List missionary support and special offerings.

Savings: List money set aside for emergencies. Indicate withdrawals with brackets [ ].

When the monthly budget amounts are completed, compute the totals. First, work from left to right, adding up annual total for each category. The annual totals added together, excluding income, can be more than, equal to or less than the total annual income. Figure the average monthly total for each category by dividing each annual total by twelve.

Personal Finances Budget Sheet Example

Category	January	February	March	April	May	June	July	August	September	October	November	December	Annual Total	Av. Monthly Total
Income - Husband	1500	1500	*1875	1500	1500	*1875	1500	1500	*1875	1500	1500	*1875	19,500	1,625
Wife	550	550	*688	550	550	*688	550	550	*688	550	550	*688	7,150	596
Tithe	205	205	256	205	205	256	205	205	256	205	205	256	2,665	222
Federal Tax (16.9%)	346	346	433	346	346	433	346	346	433	346	346	433	4,500	375
State Tax (2.1%)	44	44	54	44	44	54	44	44	54	44	44	54	568	47
County Tax (1%)	20	20	26	20	20	26	20	20	26	20	20	26	265	22
Investment (FICA)	164	164	205	164	164	205	164	164	205	164	164	205	2,130	178
Mortgage	—	—	—	—	—	—	—	—	—	—	—	—	—	—
Rent	375	375	375	375	375	375	375	375	375	375	375	375	4,500	375
Maintenance	—	—	—	—	—	—	—	—	—	—	—	—	—	—
Electricity	63	63	63	63	63	63	63	63	63	63	63	63	756	63
Heat	—	—	—	—	—	—	—	—	—	—	—	—	—	—
Water	—	—	—	—	—	—	—	—	—	—	—	—	—	—
Sewer	—	—	—	—	—	—	—	—	—	—	—	—	—	—
Disposal	—	—	—	—	—	—	—	—	—	—	—	—	—	—
Telephone	29	29	29	29	29	29	29	29	29	29	29	29	345	29
Food & Supplies	244	244	244	244	244	244	244	244	244	244	244	244	2,928	244
Clothing	50	50	50	50	50	50	50	50	50	50	50	50	600	50
Auto Payment/Lease	—	—	—	—	—	—	—	—	—	—	—	—	—	—
Auto Gas/Oil	85	85	85	85	85	85	85	85	85	85	85	85	1,020	85
Auto Insurance	—	—	500	—	—	—	—	—	—	500	—	—	1,000	83
Auto License/Reg.	—	—	—	—	—	63	—	—	—	—	—	—	63	5
Auto Maintenance	50	50	50	50	50	50	50	50	50	50	50	50	600	50
Medical/Dental	56	56	56	56	56	56	56	56	56	56	56	56	672	56
Gifts	19	19	19	19	63	19	19	19	19	63	125	125	525	44
Stationery	10	10	10	10	10	10	10	10	10	10	10	10	120	10
Dining	38	—	—	38	—	—	38	—	—	38	—	—	152	13
Travel/Vacation	—	—	—	—	—	—	—	250	200	—	—	—	450	38
Rec./Entertainment	19	19	19	19	19	19	19	19	19	19	19	19	228	19
Miscellaneous	—	—	113	—	—	—	—	113	—	—	—	113	339	28
Education	—	—	—	—	—	—	—	—	—	—	—	—	—	—
Subscriptions	—	25	—	—	—	—	—	—	—	—	—	—	25	2
Life Insurance	—	—	—	—	45	—	—	—	75	—	—	—	120	10
Debt	—	—	—	—	—	—	—	—	—	—	—	—	—	—
Unexpected Expenses	—	—	—	—	—	—	1250	—	—	—	—	—	1,250	104
Giving - missionary	25	25	25	25	25	25	25	25	25	25	25	25	300	25
Savings	210	223	453	[290]	159	503	[1040]	[115]	290	[334]	141	346	545	44
Cumulative Savings	210	433	885	595	754	1256	216	101	391	58	199	545		

[] indicates withdrawal; * indicates the months with five Fridays; Husband and wife are paid weekly on Fridays; Husband earns $9.38 per hour, 40 hours per week. Wife earns $6.88 per hour, 20 hours per week. They have no children.

Personal Finances Budget Sheet

Category	January	February	March	April	May	June	July	August	September	October	November	December	Annual Total	Av. Monthly Total
Income - Husband														
Wife														
Tithe														
Federal Tax														
State Tax														
County Tax														
Investment (FICA)														
Mortgage														
Rent														
Maintenance														
Electricity														
Heat														
Water														
Sewer														
Disposal														
Telephone														
Food & Supplies														
Clothing														
Auto Payment/Lease														
Auto Gas/Oil														
Auto Insurance														
Auto License/Reg.														
Auto Maintenance														
Medical/Dental														
Gifts														
Stationery														
Dining														
Travel/Vacation														
Rec./Entertainment														
Miscellaneous														
Education														
Subscriptions														
Life Insurance														
Debt														
Unexpected Expenses														
Giving - missionary														
Savings														
Cumulative Savings														

Personal Finances Budget Sheet

Category	January	February	March	April	May	June	July	August	September	October	November	December	Annual Total	Av. Monthly Total
Income - Husband														
Wife														
Tithe														
Federal Tax														
State Tax														
County Tax														
Investment (FICA)														
Mortgage														
Rent														
Maintenance														
Electricity														
Heat														
Water														
Sewer														
Disposal														
Telephone														
Food & Supplies														
Clothing														
Auto Payment/Lease														
Auto Gas/Oil														
Auto Insurance														
Auto License/Reg.														
Auto Maintenance														
Medical/Dental														
Gifts														
Stationery														
Dining														
Travel/Vacation														
Rec./Entertainment														
Miscellaneous														
Education														
Subscriptions														
Life Insurance														
Debt														
Unexpected expenses														
Giving - missionary														
Savings														
Cumulative Savings														

Sexual Relations

Premarital Session Five

God is the creator of sex. He originated lovemaking between married partners. Sex is "a beautiful and intimate relationship shared uniquely by a husband and wife," as stated by Tim and Beverly LaHaye in their book *The Act of Marriage*.

In His Word, God has given much information and many directions about sexual relations. He does not consider sex an embarrassing topic. He addresses marriage in a discreet and wholesome way.

God wants you to go into marriage informed about and prepared for sexual relations. God's desire is that you anticipate and then enjoy this wonderful aspect of the marriage relationship. Videos, books and audio tapes on the subject of sexual relations are available to the church today and are authored by knowledgeable and dedicated Christians. Take advantage of these resources to help you understand God's intent for sexual relations.

Exercises will provide a scriptural look at sex in marriage, questions for discussion, a self-examination of attitudes and beliefs, sexual anatomy identification and some practical information that will help you to become a caring and creative lover.

Finally, you will find helpful information about birth control in Appendix C and honeymoon precautions in Appendix D. Answers to the matching questions, the anatomy diagram and the true or false statements are found in Appendix E.

Sex in Marriage

A Look at the Scriptures

Express briefly, in your own words, what each of the following Scriptures reveals concerning attitude, reproduction, communication and sexual pleasure within the boundaries of marriage.

Genesis 2:24-25—What will leaving parents and being united to your spouse bring forth? _____

_____

_____

Genesis 1:28; Deuteronomy 7:13-14; Psalm 127:3-5; 139:13-15—What is the blessing physical oneness can produce between a husband and wife?

_____

_____

_____

_____

Song of Solomon 4:1-12; Proverbs 5:15-21; 1 Corinthians 7:2-5— How is sexual pleasure a part of God's purpose for marriage? _____

_____

_____

Hebrews 13:4; 1 Corinthians 6:12—Are there any limitations on sexual pleasure for a married couple? _____

_____

_____

Questions for Discussion

Answer the following questions to the best of your ability according to your perceptions, without the help of your fiancé. Use an additional sheet of paper if necessary.

1. Do you feel that being Christians would make any difference in your sexual relationship? _____
   _____

2. Will you be able to discuss with your spouse what you do not know about sexual relations? _____
   _____

3. What worries you or preoccupies you concerning your sexual relationship?
   _____
   _____
   _____

4. After marriage, how do you expect to communicate your desire to have sexual intercourse? _____
   _____

5. Are there any memories of the past that would have a negative effect on your present attitude or feelings concerning your sexual relationship within marriage? _____
   _____

6. Can you recall the source from which you first heard about sexual reproduction? If so, explain. _____
   _____

7. Were you free to ask your parents questions about sex? What was their response? _____
   _____
   _____

8. Can you remember any specific attitudes or expressions of your parents concerning sexual relations? _____

_____

9. Is it possible for marriage partners to be involved in lust toward one another? _____

_____

10. Is there anything that embarrasses you concerning sexual relations?

_____

_____

11. How often do you expect to engage in sexual relations each month with your spouse? _____

_____

12. Do you have any apprehension concerning sex within marriage? If so, explain. _____

_____

13. What purpose, if any, would masturbation (self-stimulation) serve within a marriage? _____

_____

14. What type(s) of contraceptives are you and your fiancé considering? Do you agree on birth control? Who will be responsible for birth control? Have you consulted your physician? _____

_____

_____

15. Have the two of you discussed your desires to have children, including how soon, how many and how close together? _____

_____

_____

Attitudes and Beliefs about Sex

On your own, place an *A* for agree or a *D* for disagree before each statement below.

_____   1. It is not the woman's responsibility to initiate sexual relations.

_____   2. Sexual response can diminish when tension exists in the marriage.

_____   3. Sex should never be a scheduled activity.

_____   4. Sexual intimacy is important to a rewarding marriage relationship.

_____   5. Mutual orgasm always occurs with sexual intercourse.

_____   6. Present sexual dysfunction may be the result of past sexual abuse or misinformation.

_____   7. Sex should never be used as a reward or punishment.

_____   8. A couple should not hesitate to seek counseling when experiencing sexual difficulties.

_____   9. Abstaining from sexual intimacy is permissible when one partner is fasting.

_____   10. It is permissible to withhold or demand sex from your spouse.

_____   11. It is God's purpose for sex to be desirable and satisfying to both partners.

_____   12. Making excuses in order to avoid sexual relations is natural and should be expected.

_____   13. A married couple should fully communicate to each other what pleases them sexually.

_____   14. Because your body is not your own, you or your spouse can request or be involved in any kind of sexual behavior within your marriage.

Matching Questions

In the blank spaces provided beside the terms below, together or individually write the letter of the definition which corresponds from the column on the right.

1. STD _____	A.	period of greatest sexual excitement
2. ejaculation _____	B.	absence of sexual desire
3. incest _____	C.	the virus that causes AIDS
4. coitus _____	D.	inability of male to perform sexual relations
5. impotence _____	E.	external organs of reproduction
6. HIV _____	F.	periodic discharge of uterine lining
7. copulation _____	G.	refraining from sexual relations
8. erection _____	H.	swelling, firmness of penis during sexual excitement
9. semen _____	I.	surgical procedure which results in inability to conceive
10. heterosexual _____	J.	sexual intercourse
11. frigidity _____	K.	synonymous for climax
12. AIDS _____	L.	sexually attracted to opposite sex
13. menstruation _____	M.	reproductive cell of female
14. sperm _____	N.	secretion discharged by male at time of orgasm
15. climax _____	O.	venereal disease which causes sterility
16. ovum _____	P.	coitus between those of near relationship
17. sterilization _____	Q.	indulging in sexual relations with many partners
18. genitals _____	R.	acquired immune deficiency syndrome
19. promiscuity _____	S.	production and release of egg from ovary
20. orgasm _____	T.	sexually transmitted disease
21. homosexual _____	U.	having sexual attraction to persons of the same sex
22. ovulation _____	V.	engaging in sexual intercourse outside of marriage
23. fornication _____	W.	male fluid of reproduction
24. masturbation _____	X.	self-stimulation of genitals for sexual gratification
25. gonorrhea _____	Y.	same as coitus
26. abstinence _____	Z.	ejection of seminal fluids from the male urethra

Anatomy

How well do you know the proper names for male and female sex organs? The drawings on this page show one half of the human body divided in the center from front to back. Given the proper name, identify each part by its number on the diagram. In the blank spaces write each appropriate number. You may complete this exercise as a couple or individually.

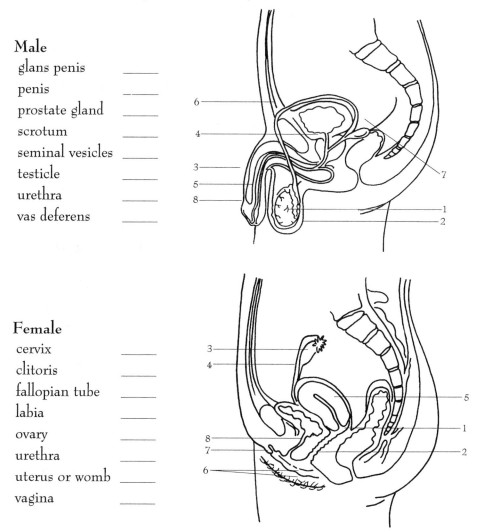

Male

glans penis _____

penis _____

prostate gland _____

scrotum _____

seminal vesicles _____

testicle _____

urethra _____

vas deferens _____

Female

cervix _____

clitoris _____

fallopian tube _____

labia _____

ovary _____

urethra _____

uterus or womb _____

vagina _____

True or False

With or without the help of your fiancé, write *T* or *F* in the space provided before each of the following statements.

_____ 1. The typical menstrual cycle occurs every 28 days and lasts for 5-7 days.

_____ 2. The foreskin is partially removed in circumcision.

_____ 3. The ova are formed in the fallopian tubes.

_____ 4. Pregnancy is most likely to occur at ovulation—14 days prior to the onset of menstruation.

_____ 5. The most common form of female contraception is the birth control pill.

_____ 6. Using a condom guarantees the AIDS virus cannot be transmitted from one partner to another.

_____ 7. When the fallopian tubes are closed by disease or surgery, pregnancy cannot occur.

_____ 8. The birth control pill prevents ovulation from occurring.

_____ 9. The scrotum covers and protects male organs that produce male reproductive cells.

_____ 10. Venereal disease can be acquired through contact with toilet seats.

_____ 11. A monogamous relationship is the best prevention of sexually transmitted diseases.

_____ 12. Herpes, genital warts and chlamydia are examples of STDs, which are increasing in incidence.

_____ 13. The AIDS virus is transmitted through semen, vaginal secretions and blood.

_____ 14. Women infected with the AIDS virus may infect their unborn babies.

_____ 15. "Honeymoon cystitis" is a common bladder infection found in newly married virgins.

_____ 16. A missed period always indicates pregnancy.

_____ 17. The sperm and egg meet in the fallopian tube.

_____ 18. Ovulation does not occur as long as a woman is nursing an infant.

_____ 19. The most sensitive sexual area of the female is the clitoris.

_____ 20. All women are negatively affected by PMS one week prior to menstruation.

A Creative Plan

Even though a creative plan cannot be implemented until after you say "I do," read and discuss these eight characteristics together with your premarital counselors. By being open and honest now, you can overcome inhibitions in becoming a creative lover.

I. Sexual Pleasure Is God's Idea

A. Sexual pleasure is God's intent for marriage. Procreation is not the only purpose for sex.

B. Sexual fulfillment is a process. It is a learned experience.
  1. Know God's intent (review the Sex in Marriage exercise, p. 56).
  2. God's desire is to encourage you and liberate you sexually.

C. Open and honest communication about the sexual relationship is necessary.
  1. Clearly communicate what is enjoyable to you.
  2. Ask what is enjoyable to your spouse.

II. Eight Characteristics of a Creative Lover

A. Be totally available (see 1 Corinthians 7:3-5).
  1. Do not deprive your husband or wife except for prayer and fasting.
  2. Schedule nights for time together. Take a nap if necessary.
  3. If you find yourself lacking sexual desire, know that right action will generate desire.
  4. What is at stake when you say no? Feelings of rejection can develop. *Note:* You can be a very loving wife or husband, but if you consistently turn your spouse down sexually, the other things you do will be negated.

B. Be carefree.
  1. Know that sexual response for a woman is tied to her emotions.
  2. Put your cares aside and freely give yourself to one another.
  3. If there is a lot on your mind, pray, then give each other a back rub.
  4. If there is hurt between you, work it out before lovemaking.

C. Be attractive. Appearance affects our attraction to each other.
  1. Always do your best to be presentable/attractive to your spouse.
  2. Don't always look "grubby" at home.
  3. Take care of yourself (shower, shave, make-up, etc.) even if you aren't going out.
  4. Wear attractive underwear. Wear attractive nightwear. Use cologne and perfume.

D. Be eager. Anticipate sexual experiences with one another.
  1. Fantasize about one another.
  2. Let God liberate you to daydream about your physical time together (see Song of Solomon chapters 4 and 8).
  3. Practice thinking about your husband or wife. Think positive things about your physical relationship (see Philippians 4:8).

E. Be creative. Study your spouse. Find out what excites him or her. What turns him or her on? Pursue creative avenues to ignite these desires.
  1. Do things differently. Be romantic.
  2. Do not try to meet your spouse's need with what you like.
  3. Do not worry about other marriages. Study your own.

F. Be interested. Do not let lovemaking become predictable and boring.
  1. You do not serve the same frozen TV dinner every night, do you? Sex will lose its interest if you are not involved in doing things differently. Communicate about this.
  2. Are you willing to make love at unorthodox times? Are you willing to try new places? Are you willing to try new things?

G. Be uninhibited (see Genesis 2:25).
  1. Adam and Eve were naked and were not ashamed. They were totally free to give themselves without inhibitions.
  2. Accept yourself—your spouse chose *you!*
  3. Do not get hung up on imperfections.
  4. Do the things that you can do. Come to terms with how you look. Don't compare yourself.
  5. Communicate with your spouse the area(s) you want to change (losing weight, gaining weight, cutting your hair, etc.).

H. Be aggressive. This advice is especially for the woman, because the man usually takes the initiative.
1. Totally give yourself—be excited, be thrilled.
2. Don't be boring and passive. Sexual relations are not just to meet biological needs.
3. Allow God to liberate you in responsiveness with consideration of your partner's feelings. Men should read First Peter 3:7.

III. **Be Involved**—follow these eight steps after marriage, and your sexual lives will blossom. Don't settle for second best. Decide to pursue God's desire of sexual pleasure in marriage.
A. Men are turned on by sight (e.g., undressing).
B. Women are turned on emotionally and by physical contact (e.g., light touching).
C. A woman is like an iron (she heats up slowly).
D. A man is like a lightbulb (he turns on instantly).
E. Foreplay must be gentle and not rushed. Foreplay for the woman must begin before the bedroom.
F. Lovemaking takes time. There may be times when we meet biological needs only, but this is *not* the norm.
G. Use proper language.
H. Be clean, brush your teeth, shave and so forth.

IV. **Sexual Oneness**—for true sexual oneness, our motive must be unselfish love toward our mate and our means must be grace. We minister to one another through unselfish, unconditional love that gives regardless of what the recipient may deserve (grace).

Ceremony Planning

Premarital Session Six

This is your special day. What kind of wedding ceremony do you want? To help you, a sample ceremony is included on pages 74-78. Try to enjoy each aspect of the planning—from choosing invitations, gowns and flowers to writing your vows and making arrangements for the honeymoon.

Your counselors will offer helpful resources for planning your ceremony and writing your vows. This session also includes exercises addressing your call together and what's in a vow. On pages 71-73 you will find a study of what takes place in the spiritual realm during the wedding. Peruse these pages carefully with your fiancé. Please direct any questions or comments to your counselors. You may also desire to discuss some of these points with your parents.

The final exercise in this chapter is a study on "submission." This exercise will bring an understanding of God's scriptural basis for government in marriage.

Do not allow yourselves to become anxious or frustrated with details. Bathe each decision in prayer. This is a one-time experience, and you will be grateful for happy memories.

Called Together?

Once again, congratulations are in order. You have completed five or more sessions in preparation for your life together. Hopefully, you now have a better understanding of the commitment you are about to make.

Perhaps you have come to the conclusion that you may not be ready for marriage. Even more painful than deciding not to get married at this point would be to spend your life feeling unsure if marriage was the right choice. If you have substantial reasons for not moving into marriage, do not ignore these convictions. Maturely and honestly acknowledge these reasons to your fiancé and counselor. Seek counsel and be absolutely sure about your decision.

Many of you, however, as a result of completing this study course, have increased desire to be married. Hopefully, you have discovered how honesty and openness cause personal growth and enhance your relationship.

Work for unity in planning your wedding ceremony. This is your special day. Here are some questions to consider together when planning your wedding ceremony.

1. What do you want your wedding ceremony to reflect to the persons attending?

   _____

   _____

2. Share several ways in which you would like to communicate God's presence in your ceremony. _____

   _____

3. How do you want those who attend to participate in this celebration with you? _____

   _____

4. Will you write your own vows?   Yes _____ No _____

5. Do you want the officiating minister to deliver a sermon?
   Yes _____ No _____   If so, what would you like to have included in the message? _____

   _____

6. Is your wedding budget reasonable?   Yes _____ No _____

7. Have you discussed this budget with your parents?   Yes _____ No _____

8. Are your parents helping financially with the wedding? Yes _____ No _____

9. Are there ways you should honor your parents in the ceremony?
   Yes _____ No _____ If so, how? _____
   _____
   _____

10. Have your parents expressed special preferences for the ceremony that you do not wish to include? Yes _____ No _____ If so, how will you deal with this? _____
   _____
   _____

Finally, do not allow the excitement of this day to rob you of creating lifelong memories. Most importantly, rejoice and be glad that two are being called together as one.

What's in a Vow?

"When a man makes a vow to the LORD or takes an oath to obligate himself by a pledge, he must not break his word but must do everything he said" (Numbers 30:2).

The dictionary defines vow as "a solemn promise or pledge that commits one to act or behave in a particular way." That obligation, promise or pledge would include your marriage vows. Marriage, according to Scripture, is a covenant to companionship. A covenant was the most binding contract in the Bible. It was an oath with great penalties if broken.

There should be no consideration given to the breaking of a marriage vow. The follower of Christ should not have a disagreement so large that it leads to divorce. Jesus said in Mark 10:9, "Therefore what God has joined together, let man not separate." The word "divorce" must be removed from our vocabulary.

Your vows are spoken to one another, to God and to those who witness your marriage ceremony. Do not take them lightly. Listen to what the book of Ecclesiastes states concerning a vow: "When you make a vow to God, do not delay in fulfilling it. He has no pleasure in fools; fulfill your vow. It is better not to vow than to make a vow and not fulfill it" (5:4-5).

What's in a vow? A commitment, a promise, a pledge, an obligation to remain married . . . "until death do us part."

Will you write your own vows? What words of commitment, value, promise and pledge do you desire to include in your vows?

Saying I Do:
What Happens at a Wedding

The marriage union gives birth to many radical changes. The least visible of these changes take place in the spiritual realm. The following is a study outline intended to point out some of those important changes. Thoroughly cover the following with your fiancé and your premarital counselors.

I. A Transfer of Authority
A. Prior to the wedding, the bride and the groom are under the authority of another.
  1. The woman comes to the wedding with her father (with whom she has spent most of her life) and leaves with her husband (with whom she will spend the remainder of her life).
  2. The man leaves father and mother to cleave to his wife.

B. After the wedding, the husband is commanded to be the authority for another, his wife. This includes spiritual leadership, as well as the responsibility to care for and draw counsel from his wife.

C. The woman changes her name.
  1. The father gives his daughter away.
  2. The bride accepts a new name.

II. An Exchange of Possessions
A. The husband and wife no longer belong to themselves. They will give of themselves in three areas:
  1. Their spirits—the most intimate area (where God dwells)
  2. Their souls—the intellect, will and emotions
  3. Their bodies—the flesh (including the skills of the flesh)

B. They give away their possessions:
  1. Automobiles, furniture and so forth
  2. Money

C. They give away their problems:
1. Physical
2. Financial
3. Relational

III. New Responsibility

A. "The head of every man is Christ, and the head of the woman is man, and the head of Christ is God" (1 Corinthians 11:3).
1. A husband is responsible to Christ.
2. A wife is responsible to her husband.
3. Christ is responsible to God.

B. As the husband is submitted to Christ, so the wife is to be submitted to her husband, allowing him to be responsible for her.

C. Husbands love your wives (Ephesians 5:25-33; 1 Peter 3:7).
1. Giving himself
2. Honoring her, being considerate
3. Giving of his name
4. Caring for her
5. Leaving past relationships
6. Living for her (dying to himself)
7. Treating her with respect

IV. New Purposes

A. To give happiness (blessing) to another and to bring fulfillment to your spouse in marriage
1. Your happiness comes from making your spouse happy.
2. Make your spouse's life meaningful.

B. To experience the fullness of being complemented by another

V. Schedule Changes

Major changes take place in individual schedules, environments or even geographical areas.

VI. Additional Relationships:

A. Marriage into the spouse's family requires special love and grace.

B. Accept and reach out to meet the needs of the in-laws.

C. Involve yourself with the friends of your spouse, and accept friendships you have brought into the marriage.

D. Additional relationships will come after having children.

VII. Wider interests:

A. As you receive the abilities, interests and areas of expertise of your spouse, they become increasingly beneficial to you.

B. As your spouse grows, rather than losing your identity, you become enriched by what your spouse adds to your relationship.

C. Interests should become mutually beneficial.

D. Each mate is a lifetime study; you continually study your mate to know him/her and to understand his/her needs.

E. Everything your mate is, knows and is becoming is yours to share.

Adapted from the radio broadcast series, "What Happens at a Wedding," David Mains and Ted Place, October 10-15, 1989. Copyright 1989 by The Chapel of the Air, Inc. Used by permission.

Sample Ceremony

The following marriage ceremony can help you begin planning your own special day. It includes the basic structure of a Christian wedding, as well as traditions found in many weddings. Ask the Holy Spirit to guide you as you creatively plan your marriage ceremony.

The Marriage Ceremony of
Mark Richard Windsor and Victoria Anne Chancery
February 14
11:00 a.m.

Prelude   (10:40 a.m.)
This Is the Day
Together as One
Make Us One
Great Is the Lord (Mark escorts in his parents as the pastor, Henry, Tom and Jeff enter from the side door.)

Processional   (11:00 a.m.)
Joyful, Joyful (Bridesmaids enter)
Bridal Chorus (Victoria and her father enter)

Giving of the Bride   Pastor
Pastor: "Who gives this bride in marriage?"
Father: "Her mother and I."
(Mark steps forward. Mark and Victoria face the front.)

Prayer   Pastor
"I ask that the congregation remain standing as we come before the Lord in prayer." (Say the prayer.)
"The congregation may be seated."

Message (10-15 minutes)   Pastor
(Include charge of faith to couple and witnesses.)

"Wives, submit to your husbands as to the Lord. For the husband is head of the wife as Christ is head of the church, his body, of which he is the Savior. Now as the church submits to Christ, so also wives should submit to their husbands in everything.

Husbands, love your wives, just as Christ loved the church and gave himself up for her to make her holy, cleansing her by the washing with water through the word, and to present her to himself as a radiant church, without stain or wrinkle or any other blemish, but holy and blameless. In this same way, husbands ought to love their wives as their own bodies. He who loves his wife loves himself. After all, no one ever hated his own body, but he feeds and cares for it, just as Christ does the church—for we are members of his body. 'For this reason a man will leave his father and mother and be united to his wife, and the two will become one flesh.' This is a profound mystery—but I am talking about Christ and the church" (Ephesians 5:22-32).

To Groom: "Have you received Jesus Christ as Lord and Savior of your life?"
Response: "I have."

To Bride: "Have you received Jesus Christ as Lord and Savior of your life?"
Response: "I have."

"The Bible tells us that any man who is in Christ is a new creation; old things have passed away and all things have become new. Mark and Victoria, your expression of faith makes you one with Jesus Christ!"

To You As Witnesses
"To the congregation, as well as to the world, I announce that Mark and Victoria stand before you cleansed by the shed blood of their personal Savior, Jesus.

"Jesus said in the eighteenth chapter of Matthew's Gospel, *'Again, I tell you that if two of you on earth agree about anything you ask for, it will be done for you by my Father in heaven.'* (18:19)

"You as a congregation are here to bear witness of this marriage. You are also here to stand before God in agreement with this union. Mark and Victoria desire your blessing upon their call together."
(Mark and Victoria move up onto platform.)

Profession of Vows   Pastor

To Groom: "Mark, do you take Victoria to be your wife, to be one with your flesh, to love her as Christ loves the church, to be faithful to her the remainder of your life?"
Response: "I do."
To Groom: "Please turn to Victoria and make this profession of your faith to her."
(Hand card to Mark. He reads it.)
Groom: "I, Mark, take you, Victoria, to be my wife. I promise before God and these witnesses to be your loving and faithful husband, in plenty and in want, in joy and in sorrow, in adversity and in health, as long as we both shall live."

To Bride: "Victoria, do you take Mark to be your husband, to be one with his flesh, submitting yourself to him as unto the Lord, showing reverence to him as the head of this union for the remainder of your life?"
Response: "I do."
To Bride: "Please turn to Mark and make this profession of your faith."
(Hand card to Victoria. She reads it.)
Bride: "I, Victoria, take you, Mark, to be my husband. I promise before God and these witnesses to be your loving and faithful wife, in plenty and in want, in joy and in sorrow, in adversity and in health, as long as we both shall live."

Presentation of the Rings   Pastor
(Get rings from best man)
"May I have the rings please? This ring is a cherished symbol—an outward expression of your faith and a token of your love to one

another. This ring is made of gold, a precious metal. It is a perfect, never-ending circle that symbolizes the continuing love of God and the gift of eternal life. These rings serve as a reminder of God's love for you, your love for one another and the commitment you are making to one another today."

(Give Victoria's ring to Mark)

To Groom: "Mark, take this ring, place it on Victoria's finger, and as you do, repeat this confession of faith to her:

"With this ring, I thee wed. I give it as a token of my faith and my love, in the name of Jesus."

(Give Mark's ring to Victoria)

To Bride: "Victoria, take this ring, place it on Mark's finger, and as you do, repeat this confession of faith to him:

"With this ring, I thee wed. I give it as a token of my faith and my love, in the name of Jesus."

Pronouncement   Pastor

"Join right hands please." (Pastor puts hand on Mark's and Victoria's hands.) "By the authority vested in me as a representative of Jesus Christ and as a minster of His gospel, and in the name of the Father, of His Son Jesus and by the power of the Holy Spirit of God, I now pronounce you united together as husband and wife. What God has joined together, let no man put asunder! You may kiss the bride."

(Music begins immediately after the kiss)

Lighting of the Unity Candle   (While song *Author of Love* plays)

Communion   Pastor

"Mark and Victoria believe it is important to seal their marriage by sharing communion together. Mark and Victoria serve a living God. Jesus Christ, who has risen from the dead, gives us resurrection power. As you eat this bread and drink this cup, you are again receiving by faith the resurrection power of Jesus Christ to be the husband and wife God has called you to be."

(Give the bread and juice)

Song *(Our Desire)*

Prayer and Blessing Pastor

"May the God who gives endurance and encouragement give you a spirit
of unity among yourselves as you follow Christ Jesus, so that with one
heart and mouth you may glorify the God and Father of our Lord Jesus
Christ.

Accept one another, then, just as Christ accepted you, in order to
bring praise to God" (Romans 15:5-7).
(Mark and Victoria turn and face the congregation)

Presentation of the Bride and Groom Pastor

"Ladies and gentlemen, I present to you Mr. and Mrs. Mark Windsor!"

Recessional *(Hallelujah Chorus)*

Mark and Victoria exit. Bridal party follows. Ushers come forward.

Pastor signs marriage license and returns vow cards.

Honeymoon Expectations

The honeymoon is a special time. Everyday life is set aside so the two of you are free to enjoy each other. It is important to keep in mind that your focus is not on the things you will be doing, but on the time you will spend together making memories. It should be a time so significant that you will enjoy reminiscing about it for the rest of your lives.

This is where expectations come in. Do you expect the honeymoon to be perfect? Will it be without a disagreement or quarrel? Will it be 100 percent romantic? Of course, neither one of you could become sick. . . .

Here are some questions for you to respond to concerning the honeymoon:

1. Why am I looking forward to our honeymoon? _____
   _____
   _____

2. What are my apprehensions concerning our honeymoon? _____
   _____
   _____

3. What if the weather does not cooperate? _____
   _____
   _____

4. What if our travel plans go awry? _____
   _____
   _____

5. What if the menstrual period occurs during our honeymoon? _____
   _____
   _____

6. Are we in agreement with what we are doing, where we are going and how long a honeymoon we are taking? _____
   _____

7. Have you scheduled your wedding ceremony early enough in the day so that your wedding night does not begin too late? _____

_____

8. When will we schedule our second honeymoon? _____

_____

_____

Probably the sexual relationship comes to mind most often when a couple thinks of their honeymoon. Expectations in this area can lead to much disappointment or unexpected satisfaction. Please keep in mind that learning to respond to each other sexually is a lifelong process. What you experience on the your wedding night and throughout your honeymoon should be unique to you as a couple.

After your honeymoon, be prepared to step back into everyday life with jobs, schedules and demands being placed upon you. Your honeymoon needs to serve as the foundation for maintaining romance and closeness throughout your Christ-centered marriage. And remember, when you do have disagreements, it will be your opportunity to put into practice what you have learned throughout the premarital program and to experience the beauty of forgiveness and healing.

God's Government in Marriage

The Value of Submission

Before working through this exercise, take a minute to write your personal definition of submission.

_____

_____

_____

_____

_____

_____

God has given man authority over the fish of the sea, the birds and every living creature (Genesis 1:28). God placed man in the garden to work and care for His creation (Genesis 2:15). From the beginning, God has established an order to things. He is not without government. Think of what this world would be like without God's management.

God's scriptural basis for order in the Christian marriage is found in Ephesians 5:21-33. Please take time to read these Scriptures. What do we see about God's government in these Scriptures?

1. Men and women are equal in God's eyes, but serve different functions within marriage.
2. The husband is positionally the "head" of the wife. He is the responsible one: responsible to love his wife (5:25); responsible to give up his life to his wife (5:25); responsible to present his wife to the Lord holy and cleansed (5:26-27); responsible to love and nurture her as he does himself (5:28); responsible to leave father and mother and become one flesh (5:31).

3. The wife is to submit to her husband (5:22). She is likened to the body of Christ. The body of Christ responds in loving submission to Christ (5:22-23). As a wife she is to respond to her husband's love (as Christ loved the church), receive his cleansing and become one flesh (5:25-26, 31). She is to respect her husband (5:33).

4. Submission: What is it? The prefix "sub" means "under." The root word is "mission." Therefore the meaning of submission is to be under the mission.

5. Does the husband force the submission of the wife? No! God spoke these words. It is God who commands, first, "submit to one another . . . " (Ephesians 5:21) and, second, "wives, submit to your husbands as to the Lord" (Ephesians 5:22). Both uses of the word imply that the one doing the submitting is choosing to place himself or herself under the authority of another.

6. The Greek word for submission in Ephesians 5:21-22 is *hupotasso*. *Hupotasso* is primarily a military term. *Hupo* means "under" and *tasso* means "arrange." Since Christ has a mission, then men are in sub-mission to Christ's mission. If the husband has a mission, then the wife is in sub-mission to her husband's mission. The man is not more important than the woman, but he is the one responsible before God to be clear on the mission.

7. "Under" does not mean "less than." Imagine a bridge spanning a river valley. Is the bridge merely a road crossing over the water? If it is, it won't stand for long! An extensive support structure *under* the bridge is essential for it to function.

8. Now imagine a train chugging across a prairie. Can the train go anywhere without a track underneath it? Of course not; one cannot function without the other. There can be no attitude of superiority in the husband or the wife.

9. Men, are you clear in your mission? If you are not clear, how can your wife be clear in her role of submission?

10. Let's look at First Peter 3:1-7 to get a better idea of the structure versus the support structure:

> Wives, in the same way be submissive to your husbands so that, if any of them do not believe the word, they may be won over without words by the behavior of their wives, when they see the purity and reverence of your lives. Your beauty should not come from outward adornment, such

as braided hair and the wearing of gold jewelry and fine clothes. Instead, it should be that of your inner self, the unfading beauty of a gentle and quiet spirit, which is of great worth in God's sight. For this is the way the holy women of the past who put their hope in God used to make themselves beautiful. They were submissive to their own husbands, like Sarah, who obeyed Abraham and called him her master. You are her daughters if you do what is right and do not give way to fear.

Husbands, in the same way be considerate as you live with your wives, and treat them with respect as the weaker partner and as heirs with you of the gracious gift of life, so that nothing will hinder your prayers.

11. According to verse 7, men are to honor the woman as the weaker vessel. This does not mean the "less than" vessel. It does not say that the woman is weaker, but we are to honor her as the weaker. Physiologically, we know women generally tire more quickly and carry less oxygen in their blood than men. But, if there is a weaker vessel, there must be a *weak* vessel as well.

12. God's plan requires the wife to submit and the husband to love. Submitting and loving both require continuous repeated action.

    God has a government. His management of the male/female role is superior to any other system of management. God's order is to cover everyone through His love. "Now I want you to realize that the head of every man is Christ, and the head of the woman is man, and the head of Christ is God. . . . In the Lord, however, woman is not independent of man, nor is man independent of woman. For as woman came from man, so also man is born of woman. But everything comes from God" (1 Corinthians 11:3, 11-12).

13. Originally, God created woman from man. Now, man is born of woman. We are not independent of the other. In God's sight, we are equal. Let's face the facts: without woman, none of us would even be here. We are equal, but not the same. "There is neither Jew nor Greek, slave nor free, male nor female, for you are all one in Christ Jesus" (Galatians 3:28). We need one another.

After the Ceremony

After the Ceremony

Postmarital training is almost unheard of. But why shouldn't we have it? The first year of marriage is foundational. There are so many adjustments to make, so many questions that arise. If the premarital instruction was helpful to you, think about how effective the reinforcement of those principles could be, along with accountability to a Christian couple, after you've said, "I do."

God encourages one full year of foundation building. His Word states in Deuteronomy 24:5, "If a man has recently married, he must not be sent to war or have any other duty laid on him. For one year he is to be free to stay at home and bring happiness to the wife he has married."

This course can be studied by those newly married or by those who have been married for some time and would like to evaluate their relationship.

Congratulations!

ongratulations are in order again now that you have become one in Jesus Christ.

This postmarital course is designed to help you build a firm foundation for your marriage. Please complete the following exercises before postmarital session number one (Three Months) and session number two (Nine Months). Take your assignments seriously and please be honest. If there are areas of conflict within your marriage there will be no better time than now to pray and work through them.

If personality profiles were used in your premarital counseling, bring them along with your *Called Together* manuals to postmarital session number one. Do not hesitate to ask any question of your postmarital counselors. They are ready and willing to serve you.

"Haven't you read . . . 'For this reason a man will leave his father and mother and be united to his wife, and the two will become one flesh'? So they are no longer two, but one. Therefore what God has joined together, let man not separate" (Matthew 19:4-6).

God bless you, as you've been called together!

Three Months

Postmarital Session One

Ninety days have come and gone since you spoke that sacred marriage vow to one another. Hopefully it has been the best ninety days of your life. Ninety days seems to be a key term in our society. We hear, for example, the following: "Full refund within ninety days if not completely satisfied"; "No interest for ninety days"; "Ninety days same as cash." What is being communicated is that in ninety days, reality begins to set in.

You have a lifetime to fulfill your commitment to your partner. The honeymoon does not need to come to an end after ninety days. You will begin to learn that romance is a vital element in keeping a marriage relationship fresh and exciting. Don't let your relationship grow stale. Ask the Holy Spirit to remind you of creative ways to express your love: remember special occasions; give flowers, cards and candy; write love notes. Be innovative with your partner. The "reality" is that marriage is a day-to-day commitment.

The first exercise is designed to provoke you into a more knowledgeable communication pattern, while the second exercise provides the opportunity to write about emotional needs. Scenario Response, the third exercise, will cause you to think about situations in which married couples often find themselves. You will explore ways to be "wise builders" in Firm Foundation and give thought to possible personal differences in Discovering the Differences. One of the final exercises will give you the unique opportunity to share observations about your spouse. Ways a Husband May Express Love to His Wife and Ways a Wife May Express Love to Her Husband will provide many ideas for demonstrating love to your spouse. The last exercise will give the two of you the opportunity to revisit your cooperative marriage mission statement from premarital counseling sessions.

Expanding Our Communication Knowledge

Read and study this exercise together.

James talks about two kinds of wisdom. He says: "Who is wise and understanding among you? Let him show it by his good life, by deeds done in the humility that comes from wisdom. But if you harbor bitter envy and selfish ambition in your hearts, do not boast about it or deny the truth. Such 'wisdom' does not come down from heaven but is earthly, unspiritual, of the devil. For where you have envy and selfish ambition, there you find disorder and every evil practice" (3:13-16).

Earthly "wisdom" causes conflict. Envy and selfish ambition give birth to disorder and evil practices. Envying your sister in the Lord because her husband is "more spiritual" than your husband reveals selfish ambition and produces conflict.

"But the wisdom that comes from heaven is first of all pure; then peace-loving, considerate, submissive, full of mercy and good fruit, impartial and sincere. Peacemakers who sow in peace raise a harvest of righteousness" (James 3:17-18).

Heavenly wisdom gives birth to divine order and righteous practices. "He mocks proud mockers but gives grace to the humble" (Proverbs 3:34). When you respond to your mate with heavenly wisdom (consideration, submission, love, mercy, etc.), envy and selfish ambition must flee: "Submit yourselves, then, to God. Resist the devil, and he will flee from you" (James 4:7). Furthermore, if you sow peace you will reap a harvest of peace.

James 4:1 raises the question, "What causes fights and quarrels among you?" James's answer is, "Don't they come from your desires that battle within you? You want something but don't get it. You kill and covet, but you cannot have what you want. You quarrel and fight. You do not have, because you do not ask God" (4:1-2).

Here lies the answer to why we have conflict; we want something but we are not getting it. Think about any conflict, past or present. You expressed a desire for something. You did not receive it or you were given something in the place of it. Hurt and/or anger arose within you. You were wronged, taken advantage of, not listened to or ignored.

Perhaps as a child you wanted a specific kind and color of bicycle for Christmas. What happened when you didn't get what you wanted? Suppose you ask your husband to wash the dishes while you attend a meeting. He forgets, and you have to do them the next morning before work. Suppose you ask your wife to iron your favorite shirt for an important meeting. She gets involved in a lengthy telephone conversation, and you are forced to iron the shirt yourself.

What is important now is your response. Will you become selfish and demanding, even accusing?

You may be tempted to use "you" statements, such as: "You're always on the phone." "Can't you ever cook a decent breakfast?" "You're always trying to make me into something I'm not." "You never clean the house." You may also be tempted to use "I told you so" statements: "You continually have to have it your way." "Well, I hope you're satisfied." "Maybe someday you'll learn to take my advice." If you become demanding you will be placing condemnation upon your spouse. Condemnation rarely motivates anyone to do anything. Instead, it makes people feel defensive. Your spouse will interpret your behavior as critical and insensitive and will want to accuse you in return.

These negative "you" statements must be replaced. Avoid using "you" statements when sharing how you feel. Wait until your anger has subsided, then replace "you" statements with "I feel" messages. Let's use two of the "you" statement examples to illustrate this point:

"you" statement	"I feel" message
"You're always on the phone."	"Honey, you probably didn't realize it, but I felt like you didn't care about whether my shirt was ironed or not."

"you" statement	"I feel" message
"You're always trying to make me into something I'm not."	"I realize I'm not perfect and I have a long way to go, but I really don't understand all the ways I offend you. I feel like I'm not being accepted for who I am. Can we discuss it?"

When demanding our way, we often use words that tear down rather than edify. Resist that selfish desire and submit your communication to God. As husband and wife, you need to hold one another accountable for how you make each other feel. You must have the courage to reveal how you feel through a soft "answer" in order to avoid criticizing and creating defensive attitudes.

"Anyone, then, who knows the good he ought to do and doesn't do it, sins" (James 4:17).

List some of the "you" statements that you may have spoken to your spouse and turn them into "I feel" messages.

"you" statement
                "I feel" message

_____   _____

_____   _____

_____   _____

_____   _____

_____   _____

"you" statement
                "I feel" message

_____   _____

_____   _____

_____   _____

_____   _____

_____   _____

Emotional Needs

Complete the following without the input of your spouse.

A. List ten of your personal emotional needs (examples of emotional needs include appreciation, affection, respect, trust, truthfulness).

   1. _____
   2. _____
   3. _____
   4. _____
   5. _____
   6. _____
   7. _____
   8. _____
   9. _____
   10. _____

B. List ten of your spouse's personal emotional needs.

   1. _____
   2. _____
   3. _____
   4. _____
   5. _____
   6. _____
   7. _____
   8. _____
   9. _____
   10. _____

C. Do you feel as though your spouse misinterprets your emotional needs? If yes, explain: _____

The goal is not to feel as though we must meet every emotional need our spouse expresses or has. We must first learn to look to God to have our emotional needs met. However, identifying those needs in our lives will help us to better understand ourselves and our spouse. This understanding can enable us to help meet our spouse's emotional needs.

Scenario Response

Complete this exercise individually.

1. How is the "ideal" marriage different from your marriage? _____

   _____

   _____

2. Because of a greater familiarity with your spouse, you now feel tempted to say things or do things you would not have considered saying or doing during your engagement. How will you handle this temptation? _____

   _____

   _____

Imagine the following scenarios:

3. You have taken the time to communicate some important information with your spouse. Your spouse did not hear you the first time, so you are now repeating your statement. In the middle of repeating this information a second time, your spouse says rather bluntly, "Would you stop mumbling and speak up so I can hear you?" What is your response? _____

   _____

   _____

4. You and your spouse have agreed to spend $50 per week on groceries. Your partner returns home from grocery shopping ecstatic about "all the great deals." You ask, "How much did you spend?" His/her response is, "$65." What is your response? _____

   _____

   _____

5. You have communicated a desire for sexual relations. Your spouse also seems to agree excitedly. In the middle of your evening prayer time, your spouse falls asleep. This would be OK except that this is the third night in a row this has happened. What is your response? _____

   _____

   _____

Firm Foundation

Please complete this exercise with your spouse.

Read Matthew 7:24-27. Jesus describes the wise and the foolish builders. Please describe the areas in which the two of you see yourselves building upon a firm foundation for marriage.

1. _____
   _____
   _____
   _____
   _____

2. _____
   _____
   _____
   _____
   _____

3. _____
   _____
   _____
   _____
   _____

As we discussed in the premarital counseling sessions, a vital part of this firm foundation is couple prayer. Please take the time to address your prayer life together as a couple. Secondly, what are your prayer goals for the future?

_____
_____
_____

Goals: _____
_____
_____

Discovering the Differences

Complete this exercise without the help of your spouse.

1. Have you discovered any likes or dislikes on the part of your spouse that you were not aware of before marriage? Please elaborate. _____

    _____

    _____

    _____

    _____

    Remember that Paul wrote in Second Corinthians 5:17 that we are becoming new creations.

2. Are your mate's moral and spiritual values what you thought they were before you were married? _____

    _____

    _____

    _____

    _____

    Jesus said in Matthew 6:21 that where our treasure is our hearts will be also.

3. Have you discovered any behavioral changes, positive or negative, in yourself or your spouse since marriage? _____

    _____

    _____

    _____

    _____

    Romans 15:7 says to accept one another. James 1:22-25 admonishes us to be doers of the Word.

Called Together

4. Have you discovered any habits (good or not so good) in yourself or your spouse that you were not aware of before marriage? Please elaborate. _____

_____

_____

_____

_____

_____

First Thessalonians 5:15 admonishes us to make sure nobody pays back wrong for wrong, but to be kind to each other.

5. Have you discovered any problems from your past that are now manifesting themselves in your marriage? _____

_____

_____

_____

_____

Galatians 5:1 tells us that Christ set us free for freedom's sake. God also states in Micah 7:18-19 that He delights in mercy and compassion. Ephesians 4:17-25 encourages us to put off the old and put on the new.

Perceptions of My Spouse

Below you are given the opportunity to evaluate your spouse. Be honest in your evaluation and remember that these are just your perceptions.

	Needs to Improve	Improving	Good	Very Good
1. Decision making				
2. Conflict resolution				
3. Finances				
4. Jealousy				
5. Hobbies (time balanced)				
6. Moodiness				
7. Temper				
8. Dependability				
9. Job (responsibility)				
10. Recreation (time balanced)				
11. Television (time balanced)				
12. Telephone				
13. Affection				
14. Friendships				
15. Praying together				
16. Spending time with you				
17. Relatives (relationships)				
18. Sense of humor				
19. Time with God				
20. Communication				

Ways a Husband May Express Love to His Wife

How to Convince Your Wife You Love Her

Evaluate the way you express your love to your wife. Go over this list and circle any ways you may be neglecting to show love for your wife. Ask your wife to go over the list and put a check mark in front of the ways she would like you to express love. Ask her to add other things to the list.

1. Function as the loving leader of your home.
2. Frequently tell her you love her.
3. If she does not work outside the home, give her an agreed upon amount of money to spend in any way she chooses.
4. Lead family devotions regularly.
5. Do something spontaneous and zany—don't always be predictable.
6. Share the household chores.
7. Take care of the children for at least three hours every week so she has free time to do whatever she wants.
8. Take her out for dinner or do some fun thing at least once a week.
9. Do the "fix-it" jobs she wants done around the house.
10. Greet her when you come home with a smile, a hug, a kiss and an "Am I glad to see you. I really missed you today."
11. Give her a lingering kiss.
12. Pat her on the shoulder, hold her hand and caress her frequently.
13. Be willing to talk to her about her concerns and don't belittle her for having those.
14. Look at her with an adoring expression.
15. Sit close to her.
16. Rub her back.
17. Shave, take a bath and brush your teeth before you have sexual relations.
18. Wear her favorite aftershave lotion.
19. Write love notes or letters to her.

20. Let her know you appreciate her and what you appreciate about her. Do this often and for things that are sometimes taken for granted.
21. Fulfill her implied or unspoken wishes as well as the specific requests she makes of you.
22. Anticipate what she might like and surprise her by doing it before she asks.
23. Play together; share her hobbies and recreational preferences enthusiastically; include her in yours.
24. Set a good example before the children.
25. Talk about her favorably to the children when she can hear you, and even when she cannot.
26. Brag about her good points to others; let her know you are proud to have her as your wife.
27. Maintain your own spiritual life through Bible study, prayer, regular church attendance and fellowship with God's people.
28. Structure your time and use it wisely; be on time to go places.
29. Make plans prayerfully and carefully.
30. Ask her advice when you have problems or decisions to make.
31. Follow her advice unless to do so would violate biblical principles.
32. Fulfill your responsibilities.
33. Be sober, but not somber, about life.
34. Have a realistic, biblical, positive attitude toward life.
35. Discuss plans with your wife before you make decisions, and when the plans are made, share them fully with your wife, giving reasons for making the decisions you did.
36. Thank her in creative ways for her attempts to please you.
37. Ask forgiveness often, and say, "I was wrong and will try to change."
38. Actually change areas of your life that you know need changing.
39. Share your insights and good experiences with her.
40. Plan a mini-honeymoon.
41. Give some expression of admiration when she wears a new dress or your favorite negligee.
42. Gently brush her leg under the table.
43. Be reasonably happy to go shopping with her.
44. Relate what happened at work or whatever you did apart from her.

45. Reminisce about the early days of your marriage.

46. Express appreciation for her parents and relatives.

47. Take her out to breakfast.

48. Agree with her about getting a new dress or some other item.

49. Thank her when she supports your decisions and cooperates enthusiastically. Especially make it a matter of celebration when she supports and helps enthusiastically at times when you know she doesn't fully agree.

50. Ask her to have sexual relations with you and seek to be especially solicitous of her desires. Express gratitude when she tries to please you.

51. Buy gifts for her.

52. Remember anniversaries and other events that are special to her.

53. Watch the TV program she wants to watch or go where she wants to go instead of doing what you want to do. Do it cheerfully and enthusiastically.

54. Be cooperative and appreciative when she holds you, caresses or kisses you.

55. Be cooperative when she tries to arouse you and desires to have sexual relations. Never make fun of her for expressing her desires.

56. Run errands gladly.

57. Pamper her and make a fuss over her.

58. Be willing to see things from her point of view.

59. Be lovingly honest with her—don't withhold truth that may hinder your present or future relationship.

60. Indicate you want to be alone with her and talk or just lie in each other's arms.

61. Refuse to cop out, blow up, attack, shift blame, withdraw or exaggerate when she seeks to make constructive suggestions or discuss problems.

62. Give her your undivided attention when she wants to talk.

63. Cheerfully stay up past your bedtime to solve problems or share her burdens.

64. Get up in the middle of the night to take care of the children so she may continue to sleep.

65. Hold her close while expressing tangible and vocal love when she is hurt, discouraged, weary or burdened.

66. Plan vacations and trips with her.

67. Help her yourself instead of telling the children to "help Mommy."

68. Be eager to share a good joke or some other interesting information you have learned.
69. Join with her in a team ministry in the church.
70. Do a Bible study or research project together.
71. Establish a family budget.
72. Keep yourself attractive and clean.
73. Be a cooperative, helpful host when you have people over for dinner or fellowship.
74. Ask her to pray with you about something.
75. Spend time with the children in play, study and communication.
76. Acknowledge that there are some specific areas or ways in which you need to improve.
77. Refuse to disagree with her in the presence of others.
78. Cooperate with her in establishing family goals and then in fulfilling them.
79. Be available and eager to fulfill her desires whenever and wherever possible and proper.
80. Begin each day with cheerfulness and tangible expressions of affection.
81. Plan to spend some time alone with her for sharing and communicating every day.
82. Remember to tell her when you must work late.
83. Refuse to work late on a regular basis.
84. Take care of the yard work properly.
85. Help the children with their homework.
86. Refuse to compare her unfavorably with other people.
87. Handle money wisely.
88. Don't allow work, church or recreational activities to keep you from fulfilling marriage or family responsibilities.
89. Try to find things to do with her.
90. Be willing to go out or stay home with her.
91. Be polite to her.
92. Refuse to be overly dependent on your parents or friends.
93. Develop mutual friends.
94. Provide adequate hospitalization insurance.

95. Make provision for housing and some support for your family in case you should die or become handicapped.
96. Be especially helpful when she is not feeling well.
97. Be on time.
98. Go to parent/teacher conferences with her.
99. Let her sleep in once in a while by feeding the children breakfast and, if possible, getting them off to school.
100. Frequently give in to her and allow her to have her own way unless to do so would be sinful.
101. Put the children to bed at night.
102. Be gentle and tender and hold her before and after sexual relations.
103. Don't nitpick and find fault and don't give the impression that you expect her to be perfect.

Adapted from *A Homework Manual for Biblical Counseling, Volume 2* by Wayne Mack. Copyright 1980. Used by permission of Presbyterian and Reformed Publishing Company, Phillipsburg, New Jersey.

Ways a Wife May
Express Love to Her Husband

How to Convince Your Husband You Love Him

Evaluate the way you express your love to your husband. Go over this list and circle any ways you may be neglecting to show love for your husband. Ask your husband to go over the list and put a check mark in front of the ways he would like you to express love. Ask him to add other things to the list.

1. Greet him at the door when he comes home with a smile, a hug, a kiss and an "Am I glad to see you. I really missed you today."
2. Have a cup of coffee or tea ready for him when he comes home from work or a trip.
3. Give him a lingering kiss.
4. Let him know you like to be with him and make arrangements so you can spend time with him without giving the impression that you really should or would rather be doing something else.
5. Be willing to talk to him about his concerns without belittling him for having these concerns.
6. Support him and cooperate with him enthusiastically when he has made a decision.
7. Tease and flirt with him.
8. Seek to arouse him and sometimes be the aggressor in sexual relations.
9. Ask him to have sexual relations more than he would expect you to.
10. Express yourself passionately during sexual relations.
11. Caress him.
12. Look at him with an adoring expression.
13. Sit close to him.
14. Hold his hand.
15. Rub his back.
16. Wear his favorite nightgown or dress or perfume.
17. Express your love in words or notes.

18. Let him know you appreciate him and what you appreciate about him. Do this often and for things that are sometimes taken for granted.

19. Frequently fulfill his unspoken wishes as well as the specific requests he makes of you. Try to anticipate what he might like and surprise him by doing it before he asks.

20. Play together (tennis, golf, party games, etc.).

21. Enthusiastically share with him in devotions and prayer; seek to set a good example for the children concerning their attitudes toward devotions and prayer.

22. Maintain your own spiritual life through Bible study and prayer.

23. Structure your time and use it wisely.

24. Be willing to face and solve problems even if it requires discomfort, change and much effort.

25. Fulfill your responsibilities.

26. Ask him for his advice and frequently follow it.

27. Be ready to leave at the appointed time.

28. Stand with him and support him in his attempts to raise your children for God.

29. Thank him in creative ways for his attempts to please you.

30. Ask for forgiveness; say, "I was wrong and will try to change."

31. Actually change areas of your life that you know need changing.

32. Work with him on his projects.

33. Read books or magazine articles he asks you to read and share your insights.

34. Let him know when he has to make decisions that you really believe he will choose the right thing and that you will wholeheartedly support him in whatever decision he makes, provided the decision does not violate clearly revealed biblical principles. Be his best cheerleader and fan.

35. Buy gifts for him.

36. Show genuine interest in his hobbies; watch or attend sporting events with him; listen to him sing and play the guitar or piano; attend a class he teaches.

37. Find a mutually agreeable way to keep the house neat and clean.

38. Cook creative and nutritious meals—or praise him when he does.

39. Have devotions with the children when he is not able to be there.
40. Maintain his disciplinary rules when he is not present.
41. Be cooperative and appreciative when he holds you, caresses you or kisses you.
42. Lovingly give him your input when you think he is in error.
43. Offer constructive suggestions when you think he could improve or become more productive. Don't push or preach or do this in such a way that you belittle him, but seek positive and nonthreatening ways to help him become more fully the man God wants him to be.
44. Run errands gladly.
45. Seek to complete, not compete with, him; be the best member on his team and seek to convince him that you are just that.
46. Be lovingly honest with him—not withholding of the truth that may hinder your relationship or future trust and closeness.
47. Be willing to see things from his point of view; believe the best about what he does or says.
48. Pamper him and make a fuss over him.
49. Be happy and cheerful.
50. Refuse to nag.
51. Gently brush his leg under the table.
52. Have candlelight and music at dinner.
53. Indicate you want to be alone with him to talk or just lie in his arms.
54. Give a "suggestive" wink.
55. Go for a walk with him.
56. Let him know you feel lonely when he is out of town.
57. Tell him what happened to you during your day.
58. Share your fears, concerns, joys, failures and so forth.
59. Seek to support your ideas with biblical insights and practical wisdom.
60. Refuse to cop out, withdraw, attack, exaggerate or shift blame when he seeks to make constructive suggestions or discuss problems.
61. Give him your undivided attention when he wants to talk.
62. Discuss the meaning of certain Bible passages or discuss how to improve your marriage, home, children or child-raising efforts.
63. Cheerfully stay up past your bedtime to resolve a disagreement or problem.

64. Hold him close while expressing tangible and vocal love when he is hurt, discouraged, weary or burdened.
65. Be eager to share a good joke or some other interesting information you have learned.
66. Work in the yard, paint a room together or wash the car.
67. Plan vacations or trips together.
68. Keep your family memorabilia, newspaper clippings, church bulletins.
69. Brag to others about his accomplishments and tell them what a good husband he is.
70. Join with him in a team ministry in the church.
71. Do a Bible study or research project together.
72. Keep up with family finances.
73. Help prepare the income tax report.
74. Keep in touch with your family and friends through letters.
75. Keep yourself attractive and clean.
76. Invite his friends or work associates over for dinner or fellowship.
77. Develop and use the spiritual gifts God has given you.
78. Ask him to pray with you.
79. Express how much you love the children and be their cheerleader.
80. Stay within the family budget; save some money for special surprises.
81. Be excited about sharing the gospel, celebrating answered prayer or helping other people.
82. Make a list of things that need to be done around the house.
83. Be satisfied with your present standard of living, furniture and appliances when you cannot afford to upgrade them.
84. Don't make nostalgic comments about your father that might imply that you think your father is a much better man than your husband.
85. Acknowledge that there are some specific areas in which you need to improve.
86. Appreciate and help his family.
87. Refuse to disagree with him in the presence of others.
88. Cooperate with him in establishing family goals.
89. Be unconventional in your lovemaking.

90. Tell him before he asks that you think he has done a good job. Don't be afraid of repeating yourself in commending him for what he is or does.
91. Be available and eager to fulfill his desires whenever and wherever possible and proper.
92. Begin each day with cheerfulness and tangible expressions of affection.
93. Let the children know that you and your husband agree; communicate to your children when your husband can hear (and when he cannot) how wonderful he is.
94. Do something spontaneous and zany—don't always be predictable.
95. Send cards to him at his workplace.
96. Stuff his suitcase with love notes when he travels.
97. Surprise him by cooking his favorite dinner.
98. Call him and tell him if you're going to be late from work or a meeting.
99. Read a couple's devotional together before bedtime.

Adapted from *A Homework Manual for Biblical Counseling, Volume 2* by Wayne Mack. Copyright 1980. Used by permission of Presbyterian and Reformed Publishing Company, Phillipsburg, New Jersey.

Postmarital Marriage Mission Statement

In Session One of your premarital counseling, you wrote an individual mission statement. In Session Two (pg. 27), you created a cooperative mission statement. Please copy that cooperative mission statement below.

Does this mission statement you have written apply to your marriage today or are there changes that need to be considered? Together make revisions, then re-write a new mission statement.

_____

_____

_____

_____

_____

_____

_____

_____

_____

_____

_____

_____

_____

_____

_____

_____

_____

_____

_____

_____

_____

Using your mission statement as a focal point, record your top three priorities. These priorities may include relationships, activities, spiritual service or personal concerns found within your mission statement.

1. _____

_____

2. _____

_____

3. _____

_____

Now create a "priorities" prayer list.

1. _____

_____

2. _____

_____

3. _____

_____

How can you pray together as a couple to see this mission accomplished?

_____

_____

_____

_____

_____

_____

_____

_____

Are there some goals you can develop in writing that will move you toward your cooperative mission statement?

Goal #1 _____

_____

Goal #2 _____

_____

Goal #3 _____

_____

We have a tendency to become preoccupied with the things we do in this world and we can easily be distracted from our life mission. Review your cooperative mission statement from time to time so you can maintain a clear focus and direction in your call together.

Nine Months

Postmarital Session Two

Your first anniversary is just three months away! You have been married almost a year! How are you feeling about your marriage, your spouse and the foundation you have been building for the past nine months? Are you meeting the goals you established for your first year of marriage? Are you feeling disillusioned in any areas of your marriage relationship?

This nine-month checkup was designed to assist you as a couple to reevaluate your goals, priorities, finances, communication patterns and sexual relationship. Challenge yourselves to pursue a new level of commitment in your marriage relationship as you proceed through the following exercises.

The first exercise, Differences and Similarities in Relationship, focuses on your strengths and weaknesses as a couple, while the second exercise provides a candid approach to discussing various areas of marriage. The next exercise centers on sexual relations, while the exercise titled Goals provides an opportunity to consider your goals together. Evaluate your spouse in the following exercise and then rework your annual budget. The postmarital study concludes with a discussion of the three parts of human beings and with one of the most important topics of marriage: forgiveness. Enjoy yourselves.

Differences and Similarities in Relationship

Complete this exercise as a couple.

1. Discuss the ways in which you are opposites. How can these differences strengthen your relationship? Discuss how the enemy (Satan) would like to use these differences to weaken your relationship. _____

    _____

    _____

    _____

2. What gifts does your spouse have that you do not have? _____

    _____

    _____

    _____

3. Discuss several incidents that have drawn you closer to your spouse.

    _____

    _____

    _____

4. How can you tell when your spouse is unhappy with you? _____

    _____

    _____

    _____

5. Which one of you is more task oriented? Which one of you is more relational? Discuss how this can be a strength, as well as a weakness.

    _____

    _____

6. Discuss the ways in which you as a couple are similar. How do these similarities strengthen your relationship? _____

    _____

    _____

For Further Discussion

Complete the following without the help of your spouse.

1. In what ways are you still tied to your parents? _____
   _____

2. Do you as a couple have other couples as close friends? _____
   _____

3. Do you as an individual still maintain close, same-sex friendships? Do you have a "best" friend? _____

4. Do you enjoy your job? Does your spouse support you working where you do? Do you have a tendency to bring work frustrations home with you?
   _____
   _____

5. In what ways do you feel your spouse is dependent upon you? _____
   _____

6. Is there something you do not understand about your spouse? _____
   _____

7. In what ways are you secure in your spouse's commitment? _____
   _____

8. (a) How have you attempted to change your spouse? _____
   _____

   (b) How has your spouse attempted to change you? _____
   _____

9. Does your spouse consider your feelings before making a decision?

_____

_____

_____

10. Are there any ways in which you feel as though you have failed to meet your spouse's needs? _____

_____

_____

11. Please list your first five priorities (for example: job, spouse, God, mother, children, ministry). _____

_____

_____

12. Are there any activities in your spouse's life that you feel are more important than you are? _____

_____

_____

13. Are there any ways in which you feel as though you have failed to meet your spouse's needs? _____

_____

_____

14. Have you hurt or offended your spouse in any way? _____

_____

_____

15. Is your spouse willing to admit that he/she is wrong? _____

_____

_____

16. Is your spouse willing to apologize? _____

_____

_____

17. Can your spouse accept advice/counsel from you? From others? _____

_____

_____

18. Does your spouse have any negative habits or attitudes that have affected your marriage? _____

_____

_____

19. Is your spouse still tied to his/her parents? _____

_____

_____

20. How much time do you as an individual and as a couple spend watching television? _____

_____

_____

What effect does television have on your marriage relationship?

_____ strong effect _____ average effect _____ little effect

Sexual Communication Exercise

Complete the following without the input of your spouse. Please be honest in your answers. Mark your answers by making a check in the yes (most of the time), no (seldom), or sometimes column.

	Yes	No	Sometimes
1. Do you enjoy your sexual relationship?			
2. Do you feel that your partner enjoys your sexual relationship?			
3. Do you and your partner agree on the frequency of sexual intercourse?			
4. Do you understand your partner's sexual needs and desires?			
5. Does your partner understand your sexual needs and desires?			
6. Do you make your sexual needs known to your partner?			
7. Does your partner make his/her sexual needs known to you?			
8. Do you and your partner take sufficient time to engage in foreplay?			
9. Do you avoid discussing any sexual areas or needs?			
10. Do you feel your partner avoids discussing any sexual areas or needs?			
11. Have you discussed sexual problems with anyone other than your spouse?			
12. Is it difficult for you to ask your partner to engage in sex?			
13. Do you and your partner pray about your sexual relationship?			

14. Have you and your partner studied any books on the sexual union?			
15. Is your partner affectionate with you outside of sexual intercourse?			
16. Are you affectionate with your partner outside of sexual intercourse?			
17. Do you and your partner discuss problems within your sexual relationship?			
18. Have you ever refused to fulfill your partner's sexual request?			
19. Has your partner ever refused to fulfill a sexual request from you?			
20. Are you able to share with your partner what you find enjoyable sexually?			
21. Does your partner share with you what he/she finds enjoyable sexually?			

Complete these statements.

22. Our sex life has been _____

_____

23. Sexually, I wish _____

_____

24. In the future, I hope our sex life will _____

_____

Goals

You may feel it is too soon to begin looking at life goals. But as the saying goes, "If you aim for nothing, you'll always hit it." Goals are important. In order to create a beneficial and suitable goal, four major characteristics are needed. Each goal must: 1) be well-defined; 2) it must denote a specific time frame; 3) it must be reachable; 4) and an accountability measure needs to be built into the goal, that is to say, who is going to check with us about reaching our goal?

Example Goal:

We desire to pay our home off completely within ten years (well-defined and attainable with a specific time frame). We will pay an extra $200 per month for ten years and place each year's tax return on the principal payment (the "how" is now defined). We will ask Rob's father to hold us accountable in accomplishing this goal (an appropriate accountability measure).

List, as a couple, several goals in the areas indicated. Please remember to be specific and realistic and to set a time limit.

1. Spiritual goals (example: a mission team trip, individual devotional time)

_____

_____

_____

_____

_____

2. Physical goals (example: to lose weight, to be more sexually responsive)

_____

_____

_____

_____

_____

3. Financial goals (example: to save $50 per paycheck, to purchase a house)

_____

_____

_____

_____

_____

_____

4. Family goals (example: when to start our family, number of children)

_____

_____

_____

_____

_____

_____

5. Employment goals (example: to be branch manager)

_____

_____

_____

_____

_____

_____

_____

Perceptions of My Spouse

Below you are given the opportunity to evaluate your spouse. Be honest in your evaluation and remember that these are just your perceptions. Compare your responses with your three month responses found on page 98. Is there improvement?

	Needs to Improve	Improving	Good	Very Good
1. Decision making				
2. Conflict resolution				
3. Finances				
4. Jealousy				
5. Hobbies (time balanced)				
6. Moodiness				
7. Temper				
8. Dependability				
9. Job (responsibility)				
10. Recreation (time balanced)				
11. Television (time balanced)				
12. Telephone				
13. Affection				
14. Friendships				
15. Praying together				
16. Spending time with you				
17. Relatives (relationships)				
18. Sense of humor				
19. Time with God				
20. Communication				

Personal Finances Budget Sheet

Since two incomes merge into one after marriage, it is important to once again go over the financial budget sheet. As a couple, you should now have a better picture of your financial needs and goals.

You will need to locate an appropriate time and place in order to begin reworking your proposed budget. It is a good idea to pray before you begin. Commit your finances to God and determine to work together in a financial agreement. It may take several hours of your time to complete, but maintaining your budget will be much less time consuming.

Instructions

Record the known or estimated monthly dollar figure for each category on the budget sheet. (We've included two blank sheets for you.) The definitions of the categories are listed below to help you determine the scope of each one. The completed example on page 51 will serve as a guideline.

Tithe: List your regular support (tithe) to your church (anything over 10% may be listed under the *Giving* category).

Tax: List federal, state and county taxes.

Investment: List any money invested for future care of your family (IRAs, retirement programs, home savings, etc.)

Mortgage/Rent: List mortgage or rent payment.

Housing Maintenance: If you own your home, estimate monthly maintenance costs.

Utilities: List your monthly utility costs.

Telephone: Estimate your monthly phone bill.

Food & Supplies: Include food (work and school lunches), drugstore supplies, department store sundries (toiletries, laundry).

Clothing: Estimate a monthly budget.

Autos: List auto payment(s) and the cost of insurance, driver's licenses, vehicle registration, gas and maintenance.

Medical/Dental: Include health insurance payments and money spent for medicines, medical/dental/optical checkups.

Gifts: List monthly expenses for gifts (birthday, wedding, etc.).

Stationery: Estimate the cost of postage and stationery.

Dining: List restaurant meals eaten out.

Travel/Vacation: List weekend travel and yearly vacation expenses.

Recreation/Entertainment: List money spent for family activities and sporting events (swimming, bowling, movies, football games, etc.).

Miscellaneous: List expenses not covered above (college loans, marriage seminars, periodical subscriptions, life insurance and personal debt).

Giving: List missionary support and special offerings.

Savings: List money set aside for emergencies. Indicate withdrawals with brackets [ ].

When the monthly budget amounts are completed, compute the totals. First, work from left to right, adding up annual totals for each category. The annual totals added together, excluding income, can be more than, equal to or less than the total annual income. Figure the average monthly total for each category by dividing each annual total by twelve.

Personal Finances Budget Sheet

Category	January	February	March	April	May	June	July	August	September	October	November	December	Annual Total	Av. Monthly Total
Income - Husband														
Wife														
Tithe														
Federal Tax														
State Tax														
County Tax														
Investment (FICA)														
Mortgage														
Rent														
Maintenance														
Electricity														
Heat														
Water														
Sewer														
Disposal														
Telephone														
Food & Supplies														
Clothing														
Auto Payment/Lease														
Auto Gas/Oil														
Auto Insurance														
Auto License/Reg.														
Auto Maintenance														
Medical/Dental														
Gifts														
Stationery														
Dining														
Travel/Vacation														
Rec./Entertainment														
Miscellaneous														
Education														
Subscriptions														
Life Insurance														
Debt														
Unexpected expenses														
Giving - missionary														
Savings														
Cumulative Savings														

Personal Finances Budget Sheet

Category	January	February	March	April	May	June	July	August	September	October	November	December	Annual Total	Av. Monthly Total
Income - Husband														
Wife														
Tithe														
Federal Tax														
State Tax														
County Tax														
Investment (FICA)														
Mortgage														
Rent														
Maintenance														
Electricity														
Heat														
Water														
Sewer														
Disposal														
Telephone														
Food & Supplies														
Clothing														
Auto Payment/Lease														
Auto Gas/Oil														
Auto Insurance														
Auto License/Reg.														
Auto Maintenance														
Medical/Dental														
Gifts														
Stationery														
Dining														
Travel/Vacation														
Rec./Entertainment														
Miscellaneous														
Education														
Subscriptions														
Life Insurance														
Debt														
Unexpected expenses														
Giving - missionary														
Savings														
Cumulative Savings														

Three Parts of Man

Read and study together.

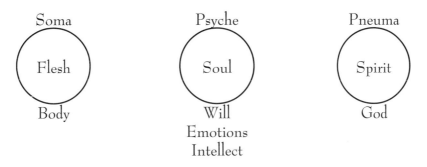

Soma	Psyche	Pneuma
Flesh	Soul	Spirit
Body	Will	God
	Emotions	
	Intellect	

We know God as Father, Son and Holy Spirit. Just as God is three in one, so is man whom He created. God has designed man with flesh, our body which will return to the dust of the earth (Genesis 3:19); soul, our will, emotions and intellect (Ezekiel 18:4; Matthew 10:28); and spirit (Psalm 51:10; John 4:23-24; 1 Thessalonians 5:23; Hebrews 4:12).

This illustration will help to clarify God's design for marriage. If the marriage is built in the fleshly realm (the lust of the eyes, the lust of the flesh—1 John 2:16, KJV) it will not endure. Before long this marriage will experience tremendous difficulty. There is much more to a relationship than the physical act of sex.

When a marriage is built in the soul realm, it may also be short-lived. Two college graduates may be able to communicate on a very intelligent level, but this alone will not be enough to sustain the relationship. If a decision to marry was made out of a strong will or during an "emotional high," this too will soon fade.

However, when a marriage is built in the spiritual realm, it is off to a powerful start. The Bible clearly indicates that God the Father, God the Son and God the Spirit agree as one (1 John 5:8). Amos 3:3 states, "Do two walk together unless they have *agreed* to do so?" (emphasis added). This agreement must first take place in the spiritual realm. Now let's look together at Matthew 18:19.

"Again, I [Jesus] tell you that if two of you on earth *agree* about anything you ask for, it will be done for you by my Father in heaven" (emphasis added). The Bible indicates that when the two of you agree it will be done. This is why a marriage built in the spiritual realm is so powerful.

If the two of you agree in prayer about a financial need, a physical need, an emotional need or a spiritual need according to God's will, it will be done. There is power in your agreement. Consequently, the key is not to argue about the need but to pray and agree.

When a marriage is built in the spirit, all of hell cannot touch it. The enemy loves to attack our flesh and our soul, but when we are built up in the spirit we need not give him any ground.

Discuss areas in which you have discovered the power of agreement with your spouse. _____

_____

_____

_____

Prayerfully list some areas in which you feel agreement still needs to be actively pursued. _____

_____

_____

_____

Can you as a couple disagree and still be in unity? _____

_____

_____

_____

_____

Forgiveness: A Final Word

Jesus taught us in Matthew 6:14-15 that if we forgive others, the Lord will forgive us. You choose whether or not to forgive. As someone appropriately said, forgiveness is God's medicine. You will feel at times that the person who has angered you does not deserve forgiveness. Jesus did not say to forgive only those who deserve forgiveness. Forgiveness releases you, as well as the one who wronged you.

Forgiveness is an important ingredient in a marriage. Anyone in close relationship with another will encounter times of stress and frustration. It is at these times that we may say the wrong thing or behave in the wrong way. The following is a practical, step-by-step, scripturally based process for forgiveness.

This exercise completes the formal postmarital training. However, it is our hope that you will continue accountability, prayer, Bible study and an ongoing desire to grow in your relationship with Christ and with each other. God bless you in your call together.

Seven Steps to Forgiveness

Anger can be a legitimate response. After the reaction of anger has been dealt with we can then move toward forgiveness.

1. Choose to forgive.

Forgiveness begins with a simple decision that, in Jesus' name, we will obey God and forgive those who have hurt us.

"Be kind and compassionate to one another, forgiving each other, just as in Christ God forgave you" (Ephesians 4:32).

Jesus made it clear in Matthew 18:35 that this decision to forgive is to be from the heart. We are to forgive wholeheartedly, not holding back or keeping any resentments.

But what about feelings? Here are some helps in dealing with them.

- Forgiveness starts not with feelings, but with a decision. You don't need to wait for the right feeling before deciding to forgive. Instead, you can forgive! You can choose to forgive from your heart, and God will recognize that. Verbalize this decision—by faith confess aloud, "In Jesus' name I forgive _____." When you have done this, your feelings will be moving toward a resolve.

- Be alert! Satan may try to bring some feelings of resentment back into your life (1 Peter 5:8-10). You do not need to feel guilty about these temptations, but you do need to deal with them. Since you have already made your choice, you need to stand firm on having already forgiven that person in Jesus' name.

- When that feeling of resentment comes back, say to yourself, "I did forgive! I dealt with that." Eventually, when you remember that sad experience, it will be with the happy thought, "That's all over." Herein lies the healing of memories.

2. Confess your sin to God.

Unforgiveness is sin against God. It is disobedience to His command to forgive others even as God has forgiven us (Ephesians 4:32). Even more, God desires for all people to know forgiveness; He sent His Son, Jesus, to die in order to make that possible. Unforgiveness can stop people from experiencing God's forgiveness. Unforgiveness is a terrible sin against God.

Yet God is always ready to forgive those who call on Him (Psalm 86:5). So accept your unforgiveness as sin and confess it to God. Do you know what He does then?

"If we confess our sins, he is faithful and just and will forgive us our sins and purify us from all unrighteousness" (1 John 1:9). This confessing implies naming our sins one by one.

"He who conceals his sins does not prosper, but whoever confesses and renounces them finds mercy" (Proverbs 28:13).

How can we be sure we are forgiven? By God's Word! He very clearly says: "For if you forgive men when they sin against you, your heavenly Father will also forgive you" (Matthew 6:14).

Yet sometimes you still doubt that you are really forgiven. There is one more thing you need to do. Receive God's forgiveness, accepting it just as you would accept a gift someone gave to you. How is this possible? Listen to what the apostle Paul said:

"We are therefore Christ's ambassadors, as though God were making his appeal through us. We implore you on Christ's behalf: Be reconciled to God. God made him who had no sin to be sin for us, so that in him we might become the righteousness of God" (2 Corinthians 5:20-21).

3. Ask forgiveness of those you wronged.

We are responsible to restore relationship with anyone who has anything against us (Matthew 5:23-24). Accept responsibility for the wrong you have done and ask for the person's forgiveness. If you do not know what you did wrong, ask God to show you.

Simply ask forgiveness. Do not go into details that would do more harm than good.

If you do not have a genuine sorrow or repentance in going to that person, stop first and prayerfully ask God to show you how you hurt that person and how he may have felt. Allow God to give you a whole new understanding and sensitivity toward that person.

It is good to look right at the person when you tell him what you did wrong and ask, "Will you forgive me?" Wait for an answer. If he says, "Yes, I will forgive," this will bring a release to him also. (Regardless of the person's answer, by confessing your sin and asking forgiveness, you have been obedient. You can now leave the situation in God's hands.)

4. Ask God to bless the person who hurt you.

"Bless those who curse you, pray for those who mistreat you" (Luke 6:28).

Ask God to truly bless the person who hurt you. And as you do this, follow the example of Jesus in asking God to bless them by forgiving them!

5. Do something nice for the person who hurt you (bless him).

"Do good to those who hate you" (Luke 6:27).

"Do not be overcome by evil, but overcome evil with good" (Romans 12:21).

This could be accomplished by complimenting that person, baking some cookies, fixing his car or baby-sitting. Ask God and He will show some act that will be meaningful to that person.

6. **Accept that person the way he is, even if he is wrong.**

Don't defend what he does, but defend him. You do not necessarily need to approve of what he is doing, but treat him with dignity, respect, love and kindness anyway.

"Accept one another then, just as Christ accepted you, in order to bring praise to God" (Romans 15:7).

7. **Look at that person through the eyes of faith and believe God to change him.**

Do not concentrate on areas of weakness, sin or irritation. Rather, concentrate on seeing that person as God wants him to be. Believe that God will answer your prayers for that person (1 John 5:14-15). Follow Abraham's example and by faith see things that are not as they appear (Romans 4:16-21). Begin to think and speak positively about that person (1 Corinthians 13:7). Love "always trusts, always hopes."

Summary

Here is a short, personalized summary of these seven steps to forgiveness:
1. In Jesus' name, I choose to forgive those who have hurt me.
2. I will confess my sins to God, especially the terrible sin of unforgiveness. (And, by faith, I will receive God's forgiveness and cleansing.)
3. I will, as God directs me, ask others for forgiveness for the wrongs I have done to them. (And I will make restitution as needed.)
4. From now on, I will ask God to bless the one who has hurt me.
5. I too will bless that person, doing kind, helpful things for him.
6. I will accept him and treat him with love and respect.
7. I will look at that person through eyes of faith, and trust God to work in him.

List below any persons that you know you need to forgive. This list may include your spouse, a parent, a friend, a coworker, someone from your childhood or yourself. You may even have a grudge against God.

_____

_____

_____

_____

_____

_____

_____

Pray over this list individually or with your spouse and be accountable to your postmarital counselors. Be sure to look back over the seven steps and see if you have completed them for each person you need to forgive.

Adapted from *Seven Steps to Forgiveness*. Copyright 1985 by Norman and Betty Charles. Used by permission of Abundant Living Ministries.

When Christians Remarry

When Christians Remarry

"**D**ivorce is absolutely the worst experience I've ever faced in my fifty-three years of life," Jim told me during a recent phone conversation. "It put my family through hell and back again. We'll never be the same."

Like a tape, I can hear Jim's words over and over again. Consider for a moment that Jim's experience is multiplied repeatedly throughout our country on a daily basis! Jim is thinking about remarriage after four years of reflecting upon a broken marriage and subsequent divorce. Jim said, "My children, three of whom are now grown, still have not recovered from their parents' divorce."

"What do you mean?" I asked.

"They haven't talked to their mother since discovering, through the events of the divorce, that she had an adulterous affair."

Four years after the event, Jim's children are still affected by his divorce. "I react to anyone who mentions the words separation or divorce," Jim says. "I challenge them to count the cost, the devastation and to seek counseling. They are often only seeing the immediate relief of the problem and the pain and are not seeing the long-term effects of divorce."

Jim is not the only one who feels this way. After completing a study with couples both inside and outside of our local church, I discovered similar concerns. Surfacing repeatedly in the surveys were such issues as children, stepchildren, husband/wife roles, problems of the former marriage, forgiveness, in-laws, finances and the church's stand on divorce and remarriage. There are many issues that relate to divorce.

Biblical Grounds

The first question for us to consider is this: "Do you have the freedom to remarry according to the Scriptures?" We live in a fallen world with a fallen nature. Consequently, there are many unbiblical grounds for divorce—even in the Church.

According to Scripture, marriage is a covenant. Through a spoken vow we made a covenant before God and before many witnesses. If there were no sin in this world there would likewise be no divorce. Divorce is the result of sin.

While the Bible clearly states that reconciliation is God's first choice (1 Corinthians 7:12-14), there are two conditions in Scripture where divorce is permitted, but certainly not required.

The first condition is that of marital unfaithfulness (Matthew 5:31-32; 19:9). The second is in the case of a nonbeliever leaving the believing spouse (1 Corinthians 7:15-16).

When Would Remarriage Be Prohibited?

God created marriage; therefore, when two people are joined together, whether they are Christians or non-Christians, it is before God. When a non-Christian marries and then subsequently divorces, he or she can be in violation of the Scriptures just as a Christian can be.

If one divorces as a non-Christian and then remarries another as a Christian, he or she is still responsible for the consequences of the first marriage. According to Second Corinthians 5:17, we are not to live in condemnation to our former sin (life), but in no way does this verse, which is often quoted by the divorced, give one a license to enter into remarriage. The idea here is that when one who has committed a murder becomes a new man through his newfound faith, he remains accountable for his "former" life of sin, albeit he is forgiven.

Andrew Cornes, an English theologian, writes, "God's absolute will is experienced in Genesis . . . it is wrong to divorce. This will of God for marriage has never been modified or abrogated. However, since men do not live up to the will of God, a law is introduced which does not commend divorce or say that it has now become the will of God . . . but which regulates it."[1]

When would remarriage be prohibited? Simply stated, when there is a nonbiblical divorce, remarriage is forbidden. Consequently, from our understanding of Scripture, if a marriage partner commits adultery and the marriage ends in divorce, then the person who has committed adultery, as the sinning partner, must choose to remain single (Matthew 5:31-32) or else perpetuate his or her sin.

A second area is found in First Corinthians 7:10-11, where Paul was quoting from the teaching of Jesus. If someone chooses to leave a marriage where there are no biblical grounds for divorce, and against the desire of his or her spouse, he or she is, as well, choosing to remain single.[2]

When a divorce occurs based upon the desertion of a believing spouse, then the offended party or that partner who has not sinned is free to remarry (1 Corinthians 7:15). Of course, in the case of the death of a spouse, the partner is free to remarry. The Old Testament Jewish practice held that if there was a right to divorce, there was a right to remarry. The New Testament teachings of Paul did not contradict this belief.

Jesus' personal stand is recorded in Mark 10:1-12 and Matthew 19:1-9. His response to the Pharisees when they questioned Him about divorce was, "What did Moses command you?" (Mark 10:3). He then made it clear in verses 5-9 that divorce was not God's plan from the beginning.

Finally, regardless of the reasons for divorce, Scripture reveals in Deuteronomy 24:1-4 that if a partner has remarried, the union is permanently broken and that reconciliation is not to be pursued. The idea of breaking up another marriage to remarry is forbidden in Scripture.

Is the question of remarriage settled in your heart with God, His word, your church leadership and with yourself? Do not make a decision based upon emotion or other people's opinions. Be sure you are clear in your heart and have the peace of God. If you do not have God's peace, it is wrong to move ahead into remarriage. If your fiancé does not have full peace, do not try to convince him or her of your opinion. You will only have regrets later. Allow your fiancé to make his or her own decision. God's Word on divorce and remarriage is clear as outlined above. As believers, we must choose to obey His Word. Obedience to God is more important than our personal feelings (John 14:21).

Divorce Statistics

Are the divorce statistics really as bad as they have been publicized and propounded to be for several decades? "Marriage as an institution is coming to an end" has been prophesied for years. But, as it turns out, the statistic which holds that one of every two marriages ends in divorce is incorrect. The *Youth Worker Journal* from September 1987 (vol. 2, no. 1) quotes a Harris poll that states, "The long-touted notion that half of all marriages fail is one of the most specious pieces of statistical nonsense ever perpetrated in modern times."

Where did the skewed figures come from? The 1981 report of the U.S. National Center for Health Statistics reported that there were 2.4 million new marriages and 1.2 million divorces that year. When that information was passed on, the most important element was frequently omitted: "A much, much bigger 54 million other marriages just keep flowing along like Old Man River." The American family is surviving.

According to the National Center for Health Statistics, the highest number of divorces take place within the first five years of marriage. This is one reason why a pre- and postmarital mentoring relationship is so vital.

God Can Identify with Divorce

How is it that God understands divorce so well? The answer is simply this: He has experienced divorce! In Jeremiah, chapter 3, we are told that Israel "defiled" the land through her "prostitution and wickedness" (3:2). Israel committed adultery (3:6), and, in verse 8, Jeremiah records, "I gave faithless Israel her certificate of divorce and sent her away because of all her adulteries."

How much God loved Israel. He extended mercy to Israel over and over again. Now, Israel's prostitution, her unfaithfulness, is more than He can bear. He will divorce Himself from such a sinful people, a people with no shame and no morals.

Have you experienced adultery committed against you? God understands. He knows how you feel because He has been there. Israel's immorality did not matter to her and the consequence was a land that was defiled (3:9). Have you felt defiled by the adulterer or have you defiled another by committing adultery?

Listen to God's words in verses twelve through fourteen: " 'Return, faithless Israel,' declares the LORD, 'I will frown on you no longer, for I am merciful,' declares the LORD. 'I will not be angry forever. Only acknowledge your guilt—you have rebelled against the LORD your God, you have scattered your favors to foreign gods under every spreading tree, and have not obeyed me,' declares the LORD. 'Return, faithless people,' declares the LORD, 'for I am your husband. I will choose you.' "

God cried out for Israel to return so He could show mercy and not remain angry because of their sins. He pleads for us to acknowledge our guilt. He then declares (authors' paraphrase), "I can't divorce you. I'm still your husband; I choose you; I love you too much to let you go." If you are still dealing with guilt, acknowledge it and choose to move on by accepting God's acceptance of you. God has called you to be free!

Trust

When a relationship is broken, trust disintegrates. Men and women who come through the other side of divorce often declare the curse-filled words, "I'll never trust again." It is understandable why these words might be spoken, but God had to move on and trust His people again, even after repeated adultery. If you do not deal with the trust issue, the small things in your next marriage may become exaggerated.

I recall a client who simply could not deal with her husband's sexual attraction to other women. To her, it represented a breach of their marriage vows, an unpardonable, unforgivable sin. Why such strong feelings? The answer was that adultery existed in her past, as well as in her former spouse's life. Now, as a newly married couple, their own experience with premarital sex added to their marital problems.

Where there is a mistrust, one will often take things too personally. When your new partner comes home from work later than he/she told you to expect him/her, the situation can quickly be exaggerated. Have you effectively dealt with the mistrust issues? Remarriage must not serve as a test to see if you have. In order to trust again, you will need to work through your hurt feelings, repent of any bitterness or unforgiveness and move to release and forgive your former spouse.

The hurt from a prior marriage can deteriorate the foundation of a new marriage. You must choose to move to a new level of trust—one of trusting Jesus in the life of the one with whom you are relating.

Fear

Fear is the opposite of love. If Satan can hold you in fear, he will be able to keep you from truly experiencing love. When fear enters a relationship, love dissipates. Fear and love cannot abide in the same home or in the same relationship. If you fear someone, loving them will be an ongoing challenge.

"Love is patient, love is kind. It does not envy, it does not boast, it is not proud. It is not rude, it is not self-seeking, it is not easily angered, it keeps no record of wrongs," states First Corinthians 13:4-5. You cannot substitute the word fear for love in these Scriptures. Try it. It will not work because, "There is no fear in love. But perfect love drives out fear, because fear has to do with punishment. The one who fears is not made perfect in love" (1 John 4:18).

Fear can play a major role in remarriage. If one marriage has failed, it certainly stands to reason that another could fail. This is fear. If one spouse has sinned, another could sin. Again, the motivation is fear. Just because someone says he/she is a Christian does not mean he/she will not change and become a different person—fear.

Does fear grip you? Then it is time to fall out of fellowship with fear and be renewed in Jesus' love. Remember the verse "Perfect love drives out fear"? Take authority over fear in your life in Jesus' name. Drive it out by the power of the blood of Jesus and put on His robe of love so you can be free from fear.

Fear can keep you from a wholehearted commitment to a new relationship. Having "broken" one vow, it is easy to think about breaking another. It is important to understand that there needs to be a solid commitment "for the remainder of our lives on this earth" to weather all the challenging storms that may be ahead.

If fear or mistrust tries to come between you and the one you love, share the thought or the feeling immediately. Do not allow it to fester in your mind. Satan will attempt to exaggerate that fear or mistrust. After you share, pray together. Drive the fear or the mistrust out with honesty, accountability and prayer.

Reprogramming

Thomas J. Watson, the former president of IBM, once said, "It's a common mistake to see failure as the enemy of success. Failure is a teacher—a harsh one, but the best."

How did you fail in your first marriage? Have you received personal counseling to help you admit your failures, talk them through, repent and develop new and redeemed life patterns? If not, you will see these failures repeated. If you failed at communication, what have you learned? If you failed at role responsibility, how do you see roles differently? The bottom line is that you must take an honest and deep look at yourself.

Failure to do this keeps you in denial and blame. The result will be no spiritual or emotional growth and maturity on your part.

The number one reason for failure of marriages is selfishness—we want what we want (James 3:13-18; 4:1-3). Have you matured beyond this? Can you remove the shaded glasses of mistrust, immaturity, guilt, rejection and selfishness from your eyes?

Can you put on the life of Christ who came in the form of a servant? "Who, being in very nature God, did not consider equality with God something to be grasped, but made himself nothing, taking the very nature of a servant, being made in human likeness" (Philippians 2:6-7).

Can you reprogram that old way of thinking about marriage, about sex, about money, about your needs? It is vital to confront these old patterns of thinking. Romans 12:2 says that we are to be "transformed by the renewing of [our] mind." Have you sincerely asked the Lord to expose wrong thinking from past relationships? I encourage you to do this now.

Write down some of those misbeliefs (wrong thoughts) you've brought with you from your former marriage. As you record them, ask the Lord to reveal the truth of Scripture to replace the wrong thinking. Review the Knowing Who You Are in Christ worksheet found in Session One of *Called Together*. Renew your mind with truth, not the lies from the past.[3]

Children and Stepchildren

How do you love a child who is not yours? Will this child accept you? If both of you are bringing children into a new marriage union, how will they get along?

The subject of children was the most frequently discussed topic in our surveys with remarried couples. The unanticipated adjustments for the children and their parent who was remarrying provoked the most problems for these couples.

The Fresh Start Divorce Recovery Workbook, from Thomas Nelson Publishers, lists three reasons for this difficult transition:[4]

In the children's minds . . .

1. It ends the fantasy that their parents might get back together.
2. It triggers the fear that the new spouse will take away the love their parent has for them.
3. It creates anxiety about whether they will get along with this intruder in their family.

Children need time to heal from a divorce. Their own feelings of hurt, rejection, separation anxiety, fear and anger must be talked about. If this outlet of healing is not provided, parents will find tension and strife in their relationships with their children.

It will take time to bond with stepchildren. Older children can be very resistant to this process. They feel the loss of a parent more than they feel the excitement of a having a new parent. It is strongly advised that the children enter the process of premarital counseling. This will help to deal with some of these issues before a remarriage takes place.

Allow the children time to accept the changes forthcoming and to develop a relationship with the stepparent. Don't expect immediate acceptance. Ask what the children prefer to call the stepparent. Be prepared to be rejected. Do not retaliate with rejection on your part.

Never try to compete with the ex-spouse's relationship with his or her child. This will not impress the stepchild and may cause even more distance. As they sense their parent's loyalty moving toward a stepparent-to-be, their communication may decrease. Individual counseling for the children may be advisable.

Along with the emotions listed above, here are some topics to consider addressing with children in premarital counseling: discipline (new/old rules), parental roles, parental authority, visitation and changes in such areas as school, residence, bedroom arrangements, sports, jobs and finances.

No matter how fairly you try to treat your children, you will most likely see your children, your spouse's children and any children born to this new union differently. Although you may have the same goal for all of the children, how you treat each one will take tremendous grace. This grace will allow Christ-centered blended families to experience happiness and unity.

Maintain Your Focus

Today in the United States, the family focus has become the children. This should not be the case. The focus needs to be the marriage. A child-centered focus disrupts marital unity and agreement. The marriage will need to be stable and healthy after the children have left home. Many couples do not have a relationship left after the children are raised because their focus is out of balance.

Children (especially children from blended families) need security. Security, however, does not come from purchasing lots of material things (Nintendo®, computers, cars, etc.). Security does not come from our children being able to attend every extra-curricular school activity or every friend's party. Security for children is a product of Mom and Dad loving each other and prioritizing God's principles in their marriage. Ask any child: Would you prefer Mom and Dad to stay married and work on their relationship, or would you like the newest, the best, the most expensive _____? Children want their parents to stay together.

Goals and Vision

Why are you considering remarriage? Why this person? What is the goal, the vision of this marriage? If you are considering remarriage for the sake of convenience, for providing a parent to your children, for financial help, to take care of loneliness or just because you want to remarry, then you are treading on thin ice. These are not reasons for remarriage.

Marriage is for the mature. Only mature people can maintain a lifetime commitment. Marriage changes a person's status, not the person. Are you overlooking something in your fiancé's life that you think will change when you marry? Are you compromising on your personal standards in any way by considering this person? If the answer to either of these questions is "yes," then you are involved in immature thinking and are not facing reality.

If your answer is "no," then move on to these questions: Why is God calling us together? What is His goal/vision for us? What is it in this vision that we can only fulfill by becoming married? You must discover His answer to these questions.

Other Areas to Consider

One couple I interviewed told me they had made a big mistake by moving into "his house with his daughters." Given the chance to do it over again, they would have sold both properties and moved into a new, neutral home. There are memories and loyalties connected to homes, and this potential problem could be resolved by relocating to a new property.

If you have been without a spouse for some time, please consider that you will be giving up your independence. You will be going back to making cooperative decisions and being involved in mutual submission. You will need to reconsider some of those set-in-your-ways patterns.

Consider your former in-laws, as well as future in-laws. What will the relationships be like? How will they change? What will be decided in regards to grandchildren and visitation?

What church will you attend? Will people in your church find it difficult to see you with another spouse? Will you need to consider attending a new church and developing new relationships?

Have you discussed your financial obligations? Are you aware of each other's indebtedness? Are you ready to assume this indebtedness? Have you communicated about your savings, retirement plans, life insurances, different checking accounts and credit accounts?

Are you reading books on the topic of divorce and remarriage, children of divorced parents and other related topics? See the recommended reading list in this section. You can learn so much from other people's experiences. Avail yourself of them.

Have you given yourself sufficient time to grieve the loss of a marriage? Some experts believe that no one should begin to consider remarriage after divorce or the death of a spouse within one year after the loss. Others extend that time period to two years. This all-important time factor allows you to go through the healing process, as well as the adjustments. If you have children, they need this time to adjust as well. If a new relationship begins too soon, the children will almost automatically reject the person seeing their mom or dad.

This is not just a "get over it" or a "get back to everyday normal life" time period. It is a time to discover what "normal" is. It is also a time to work through the emotions. Divorce sends shock waves to the core of your being. You must allow sufficient time for healing and adjusting.

Finally, consider becoming a team again. Reflect on how you see a marriage team operating. How would it differ from how your first marriage operated? One couple shared with me that they began their remarriage with a competitive spirit rather than a team spirit. They needed to deal with their pride, their jealousy of one another, their differences in handling the children and even which one of them would cook the meal. As they dealt with these areas, the competitive spirit gave way to a team spirit. Eventually, they developed their own cooperative way, which was unique to them as a newly married couple.

The Final Word: Forgiveness

Jesus said, "For if you forgive men when they sin against you, your heavenly Father will also forgive you. But if you do not forgive men their sins, your Father will not forgive your sins" (Matthew 6:14-15).

Do you hold any grudges toward God, your former spouse, former in-laws, former friends, a pastor or Sunday school teacher or yourself? If the slate is not clean, you will infect this new marriage relationship with your unforgiveness.

Forgiveness is not saying that your former spouse was right. Forgiveness is letting go of the many hurts and wounds inflicted by that person so you can be healed. The healthier you are, the healthier your marriage will be. Forgiveness also means being reconciled to your former spouse in order to interact with him/her over the myriad of children's issues.

Unforgiveness is like a cancer—it spreads and it is deadly. Forgiveness is the last stage of divorce recovery and the first stage of a new view of life. It is saying good-bye to the denial, the shock, the anger, the depression, the fear and the rejection.

Forgiveness brings you into a new realm of acceptance and wholeness. Forgiving is Jesus' medicine. It comes straight from the cross. It is the blood that poured from the veins of God. It is the "Jesus factor."

Pray this prayer with me:

Dear heavenly Father,
Thank You for experiencing divorce for me and with me. Thank You for going through the pain and the rejection of separation and divorce. Thank You for Your grace, which has brought me to this place in my life. At times, I may have even felt rejected by You. I was not. At times, I thought I bore this pain alone. I

did not. And, at times, I thought my anger would change our relationship forever. My relationship with You is more secure today. You have seen me through so much. While I may walk "with a limp," it is a reminder of my inabilities and of Your abilities.

Forgive me now for holding anything against anyone. I release _____(list name[s] of the person[s] you need to forgive) in Jesus' name and commit them to You. I place them into Your hands. I thank You, Father, that the shed blood of Jesus covers my sin, as well as their sin. I declare freedom from bitterness or any lingering effects of unforgiveness. Renew my mind and my heart.

In Jesus' name, Amen.

As you have taken a step of faith by forgiving and releasing hurts from the past, know that freedom will come to have trust increase and fear decrease. God's best to you on your remarriage journey.

Endnotes

1. Andrew Cornes, *Divorce and Remarriage: Biblical Principles and Pastoral Practice* (London: Hodder and Stoughton Publishers, 1993), 189.

2. The New Testament verses on divorce and remarriage are as follows: Matthew 5:31-32; 19:1-12; Mark 10:1-12; Luke 16:18; 1 Corinthians 7:10-16.

3. For more in-depth focus on renewing your mind, see William Backus, *Learning to Tell Yourself the Truth: A Six Week Guide* (Minneapolis: Bethany House Publishers, 1994).

4. Bob Burns and Tom Whiteman, *The Fresh Start Divorce Recovery Workbook* (Nashville: Thomas Nelson Publishers, 1992). A seminar and workbook of 300 pages helps you to face the past, the present and the future concerning divorce.

Called Together

Remarriage

Premarital Exercises

Remarriage Exercises

History

Because we bring our histories with us, it is important for both of us to know whether or not we have dealt with the issues of the past. Complete the following exercise individually without the help of your fiancé.

1. Discuss some of the mistakes you made in your previous marriage relationship. _____
   _____
   _____

2. What have you done to work on the areas you wrote about in number one? _____
   _____
   _____

3. How can you demonstrate the healing you have received from past experiences and hurts? To what evidence can you point to show new patterns in current relationships? _____
   _____
   _____

4. How long have you lived without a spouse? With what areas of independence do you believe you may struggle if you remarry?
   _____
   _____

5. Were there any experiences of abuse from your previous marriage and, if so, what were they? _____
   _____
   _____

6. Since experiencing this abuse, what have you come to believe about it?

_____

_____

7. According to Matthew 7:3 (looking at the fault in your brother's eye and not considering your own), how will you handle the temptation to express in a negative manner something you see in your mate that existed in your former spouse? _____

_____

8. What interaction will you have with your former spouse? _____

_____

_____

9. Does your fiancé have a workable relationship with his/her former spouse?

_____

_____

10. What will you consider reasonable interaction for your spouse to have with his/her former spouse? _____

_____

11. Because of a previous marriage ending in divorce, how will you handle feelings of insecurity when going through a difficult time with your new spouse? _____

_____

_____

12. In your previous marriage, did you find yourself providing any type of "cover up" for your spouse?   Yes _____ No _____
If yes, please expound. _____

_____

_____

13. As you consider spousal roles, what previous roles did you play that you do not desire to play in a new marriage (for example, total caretaker of the finances, the children, etc.)? _____

_____

_____

14. What were some of the expectations you had of your former spouse that were not fulfilled? _____

_____

_____

15. What mistakes do you feel your former spouse made in marriage?

_____

_____

_____

16. For what things have you had to forgive your former spouse? Are there any areas of forgiveness you still struggle with? _____

_____

_____

17. Have you discovered what kind of person you were married to and why you chose him or her? In other words, can you identify any wrong thinking patterns from the previous relationship? _____

_____

_____

18. What good thing(s) from your previous marriage relationship do you desire to bring into this new one? _____

_____

_____

Biblical Grounds

In the following exercise, please provide your personal scriptural response.

1. Upon what biblical grounds did you base your divorce? Name specific Scriptures and your interpretation of those verses. _____

   _____

   _____

   _____

2. Upon what biblical grounds do you base your remarriage? Specifically, what Scriptures do you use to back up your decision to remarry? _____

   _____

   _____

   _____

3. Discuss how you know you have God's peace and confirmation of this relationship: _____

   _____

   _____

   _____

4. Have you sought God's forgiveness for your part in the breakup of your former marriage relationship? Have you accepted that forgiveness?

   _____

   _____

   _____

5. What do you desire to accomplish by bringing two families together in re-marriage? _____

   _____

   _____

   _____

Trust and Fear

Because trust and fear are two specific areas that affect couples who remarry, respond to the following questions individually.

1. What areas of trust were fractured in your previous marriage? _____

   _____

   _____

   _____

   _____

2. How has the Lord walked you through healing of this brokenness? _____

   _____

   _____

   _____

   _____

3. List any fears you have as you consider remarriage. _____

   _____

   _____

   _____

   _____

4. What steps will you take not to carry mistrust and fear into this new union, and what action will you take if mistrust or fear become an issue? _____

   _____

   _____

   _____

   _____

Children

Divorce and remarriage are very difficult for children. As you consider remarriage, think about how it will impact the children. Respond individually to this exercise.

1. Have your children worked through the grief and/or rejection that can occur from divorce?   Yes _____ No _____

2. What is their understanding of the broken relationship at this point of their lives? _____

   _____

3. Do your children blame themselves for any aspect of the divorce? Yes _____ No _____

4. Have your children made room in their hearts for a stepparent? Yes _____ No _____

5. What do you see as the best method to unite two families as one?

   _____

   _____

6. Discuss how you will love a child (stepchild) who is not your biological child.

   _____

   _____

7. Of the two of you, who do you believe is more strict when it comes to parenting? _____

   _____

8. Will you allow one another to correct any child freely? Yes _____ No _____

9. Who do you see as responsible to provide the primary discipline of the children?

_____

_____

10. Do you feel it is necessary for your stepchildren to follow the rules you have made for your own biological children? Yes _____ No _____
Name any examples that you can think of where this would not be the case.

_____

_____

_____

11. Finish this sentence: Accepting my fiancé's children into our home and our family will be . . . _____

_____

_____

12. Please list your methods of discipline along with sample offenses. _____

_____

_____

_____

13. What are some of your goals for your children and stepchildren? _____

_____

_____

_____

14. What are some practical ways you can guard against jealousy that your children may feel toward your new partner? _____

_____

_____

15. Will you have children together in this new union?
Yes _____ No _____ How many? _____

16. How will you handle a stepchild rejecting you? _____

_____

_____

17. What do you expect the stepchildren to call you? _____
_____
_____

18. How do you see bonding taking place with stepchildren? _____
_____
_____

19. Have you met your fiancé's former spouse? How do you view his or her parenting skills? _____
_____
_____

20. Do you and your fiancé agree with the visitation arrangements of non-custodial children?   Yes _____ No _____

21. Does your potential spouse understand and agree with any financial commitments you have concerning child support?   Yes _____ No _____

22. Will any of your children (biological or stepchildren) need to change schools, jobs, churches, activities or move away from friends or grandparents? Yes _____ No _____ How will you handle this? _____
_____

23. Have you discussed with the children a new place of residence, bedroom arrangements and/or the sharing of toys? _____
_____
_____

24. How will you take financial responsibility for your stepchildren even if their parent is receiving support? _____
_____
_____

25. Discuss with one another how you will handle the holiday season (gifts, grandparents, visitation, etc.). _____
_____
_____

Questions to Ask Your Children

Here is a list of questions for you to ask your children to respond to. Please feel free to reword the questions for younger children.

1. What are some of the things you like or appreciate about your mother's or father's fiancé? _____

2. Finish this sentence: When my mother/father remarries, I . . . _____

3. One thing I fear about my parent remarrying is . . . _____

4. An area I am excited about concerning remarriage is . . . _____

5. If you will be moving to another home, how do you feel about this? _____

6. What are some of the changes you'll need to face with a possible remarriage?

7. Do you feel you are able to communicate well with your future stepparent?

8. What do you desire to call your stepmother/stepfather? _____

9. How do you get along with your future stepparent's children? _____
_____

10. What are your thoughts about your future stepparent administering discipline
to you? _____
_____

11. What will you do when you do not agree with your stepparent? _____
_____

12. Do you feel jealous about anything relating to this remarriage (for example,
jealous of a future stepbrother or sister, jealous of someone trying to
take your biological parent's place)? _____
_____

13. Do you feel resentful about anything related to this remarriage (for example,
resentment toward a future stepparent, resentment toward your parent
for divorcing and entering this new relationship)? _____
_____

14. Have you ever felt "demoted" by your parent because he or she was pursuing
another marriage relationship? _____
_____

15. Have you made room in your heart to receive a stepparent? _____
_____

16. Is there anything else you would like to share? _____
_____

Other Questions to Consider

You may confer with one another as you respond to the following questions.

1. What church will you attend? _____

    _____

    _____

    _____

    _____

2. Where will you live? _____

    _____

    _____

    _____

3. How will you handle your savings accounts, retirements and indebtedness?

    _____

    _____

    _____

    _____

4. What problems do you feel you still need to work through in this relationship
    before remarriage? _____

    _____

    _____

    _____

5. How are your fiancé's character traits different from your former spouse's
    character traits? _____

    _____

    _____

    _____

6. Are these the character qualities you have been looking for? _____
_____
_____
_____
_____

7. Do you anticipate any former or future in-law difficulties? Please expound.
_____
_____
_____
_____

8. Is there anyone questioning whether you should remarry at this time or enter into marriage with this person? _____
_____
_____
_____

9. Where does your pastor and/or spiritual leader(s) stand as you consider remarriage? _____
_____
_____
_____

10. Are there doubts or questions keeping you from being confident about your remarriage? And are you convinced you are to marry this person?
_____
_____
_____
_____

Remarriage Interview

Find a couple who is remarried and ask them if they would be willing to communicate with you and your fiancé about some of the experiences they have had. The following are suggested questions you can ask to generate dialogue between you as couples.

1. Could you share with us some of the positive experiences you have enjoyed as a remarried couple?
2. What are some of the negative experiences you've encountered?
3. What keeps your marriage strong in the midst of differences?
4. What, if any, were areas of surprise to both of you?
5. If you brought children into this new union, what were your experiences with this blending?
6. How have you handled changes with church, finances, in-laws, friends, relocation and so forth?
7. Now that you can look at your decision in retrospect, what would you have done differently, if anything?
8. How do you handle the temptation of mentioning your former spouse or of speaking negatively of your spouse's former mate?
9. How did you handle a "competitive spirit" and become a team?
10. What books have been helpful to you?

Notes: _____

_____

_____

_____

_____

_____

_____

_____

_____

_____

_____

_____

Scenario Response

Complete this exercise individually.

1. Your spouse has just corrected "your" child differently than you feel he or she corrects "his/her" child. How will you handle this? _____

_____

_____

2. Something your spouse just did or said caused an emotion producing a flash-back of your former spouse. What will you do? _____

_____

_____

3. You just tried to joke with your spouse and he or she took offense because it reminded him/her of his/her former wife or husband. Your response to your spouse might be . . . _____

_____

_____

4. You are noticing some distance between you and your stepchild. You ask him/her about it and the reply is that there are no problems. What's the next step? _____

_____

_____

5. You and your fiance are choosing to make the necessary changes for this new union. Stepchildren may not have the same option or choice. How will you handle children who feel "forced" to blend their families with very little knowledge and experience as to what this will mean for them and their future? _____

_____

_____

_____

Progression of Healing

Before completing the Progression of Healing exercise, perhaps a bit of explanation is necessary. The purpose of this exercise is to provide a very important aspect of the remarriage process. Before you rent an apartment, buy a home, take in a foster child or change jobs, often a "background" check is required. Normally, this is someone taking an objective look at your history of payment or personal integrity. If you have been totally honest about your past, then any check on your history is not threatening.

If your credit history is important to a loan officer, one with whom you will not have an ongoing relationship, how much more important is your progression of healing to the one you desire to spend the rest of your life married to? Too many times couples have gotten into trouble with an "I love him, the past is the past" attitude, which later turned devastatingly sour when "secrets" were exposed.

So, be honest, open and willing to discover things about your fiancé and yourself that will provoke further growth in your life.

In order for your fiancé to discover how you have progressed in the healing process, please list three names of persons for him/her to contact. Preferably, these persons would have walked through your divorce with you so they can objectively attest to your personal healing process and recovery.

List names, addresses and phone numbers of persons to contact:

Name	Address	Phone Number

Things I discovered about my fiancé and myself through this process:

_____

_____

_____

_____

_____

_____

_____

_____

_____

_____

Recommended Reading

Barnes, R. *You're Not My Daddy*. Dallas: Word Publishers, 1992. (Out of Print)

Brown, B.E. *When You're Mom No. 2*. Ann Arbor, MI: Servant Publications, 1991. (Out of Print)

Frydenger, T. & Frydenger, A. *Resolving Conflict in the Blended Family*. Tarrytown, NY: Fleming H. Revell, Co., Chosen Books, 1987.

Johnson, C. *How to Blend a Family*. Grand Rapids: Zondervan Publishing House, 1989. (Out of Print)

Lehman, K. *Living in a Step Family Without Getting Stepped On*. Nashville, TN: Thomas Nelson Publishers, 1994.

Smoke, Jim. *Growing in Remarriage: Seven Keys to a Successful Second Marriage*. Ada, Michigan: Fleming H. Revell, 1990.

Called Together

Intercultural Marriages

Intercultural Marriages

Intercultural marriage adds an extra set of dynamics to relationships. More and more Christians go out of their country of origin either for short-term or long-term missions, education, employment or travel. In addition, many diverse cultures live together in the same country or city. Your neighbor may be from another culture.

Regardless of how those of differing cultures met and grew to love one another, the desire to marry comes with a need to merge two cultures into one. Many questions arise.

Will our families understand? What about spousal roles? What differences will be encountered with food and meal preparation?

Recently, we created a survey questionnaire about intercultural marriage and asked many such couples to respond to some of the positives and negatives within an intercultural marriage. The answers were eye-opening and helpful.

Assumptions: My Way— The Right Way?

Probably one of the biggest assumptions made within marriage is that the way we do things is the correct way. After all, "My family has always done it this way and it works quite well." This same assumption is found within intercultural marriages, but it's magnified.

Assumptions about how we live come with each culture. All of our life experiences through family and cultural background teach us how to deal with life's challenges. Within an intercultural marriage, many different assumptions will surface over time. We will formulate our opinions and make judgments based upon our worldviews. Initially, these judgments will be external or on the surface. In time, all of the internal areas will be exposed also. Often, this is how we begin to formulate our own prejudice against other cultures.

For example, there are banks in the United States and there are banks in New Zealand. Both banks serve a similar function, but in New Zealand you do not sign your checks to be cashed. Deposit slips are completed very differently as well. In the United States, one banking company will not cash another's check unless you have an account with them. In New Zealand, the banks tend to work together. Neither banking system is wrong; however, to the spouse encountering a new and unfamiliar system, it may be a challenge. The tendency to think, "The way we did it in my country was better," will emerge quickly and frequently. Will we recognize it or try to hide it? This is the critical issue.

Another example of differences to think about is the medical arena. Medical services differ greatly from country to country. One country may have a national medicine provision, while other countries have very few doctors and distant or poor services. The United States has medical technology that many countries do not have, but it has a higher cost and a system that requires individuals to pay their own bills instead of the government. Will this present a problem for you? Consider this important medical question: Where will your children be born and why do you feel the way you do about this?

Other assumptions may be made in such areas as home decorating, the way money is handled, unfamiliar types of entertainment, differing degrees of acceptable openness in personal sharing, different understandings of extended family relationships, the celebration of unfamiliar holidays, differing views of romanticism, the use of free time and vacations and even the way children receive their education. These areas are not meant to be all inclusive, but to give you a general idea about the assumptions we all have and would need to face in the event of an intercultural marriage.

Some of the negatives discovered by couples who are interculturally married can be quite varied. One wife confessed that her way of doing certain things drew a negative response from her spouse. For example, the way dishes are washed, the care of clothing or how the children are disciplined often varies from culture to culture. Marrying someone from an underdeveloped country and then bringing that person to the States may be shocking. The prosperity of North America can be incomprehensible. Likewise, the lack of what others may view as essentials can be equally shocking.

Adjusting to Differing Cultural Norms

Feeling as though you are expected to be like the wives or husbands of the culture you married into can be a monumental hurdle to cross. Cultural and social norms may be so diametrically opposed to your country of origin that you become emotionally confused. An inability to understand the perceived role is difficult enough, without the fact that you may not agree with the traditions.

Keep in mind that in some countries, it is acceptable for the man to marry outside his culture, but not for the woman or vice versa. This fact may make it more difficult to have a good intercultural marriage in that particular country.

One couple we surveyed shared that as a wife from North America living in Africa, it was difficult for her to get used to the lack of automatic washers in that part of Africa and to understand how African women could manage without them. A young North American wife now living in the jungle of Guatemala said, "There's no use for high-heeled shoes here in the deep mud. It took me some time to get used to this fact. I needed to learn to die to some of my personal values concerning femininity and just become real practical." Whereas, some new North American wives felt pressure to "dress up" to be accepted as feminine.

Caution 1: Know Each Other's Culture!

With each of the couples we interviewed, several cautions kept emerging. One of the strongest was knowing each other's culture. If at all possible, spend some time living in that culture before marriage. The minimum amount of time suggested was two to three months. While visiting your fiancé's country of origin, it would be important to live with a local family as well as your fiancé's family. This would enable you to experience firsthand the relationship differences within the family.

A word of caution: While you are picking up certain nuances, don't think that all families of this culture operate this way. It would be like saying all North American or European families function in a similar way.

Much can and should be learned about your future mate's culture before marriage. A wife shared with me that she never understood her husband's concept of time until she traveled to his country. "To my husband's culture, a moment may mean several hours," she explained. She went on to say that a 10:00 a.m. wedding may begin at noon.

Imagine the challenges this one concept can present. When asked how she worked this problem out, she said, "My husband learned to respect time consciousness more and I had to learn it was sometimes convenient to be late. You soon discover that relationship is more important than time."

This topic alone helped to move this couple away from "my way is the right way" to "I've learned one way, you another. Let's glean from both and discover the best way for us."

An American woman married to a man from Scotland said, "The American way of life is a very independent one. In Scotland, the people in the community are much more aware of your presence and they are more social. Family life is very different. It is a new way of thinking, and I had to discover the thought process of the new country I was now living in." Once she began to understand and appreciate the new way of thinking, she became very comfortable with this "foreign" country.

Caution 2: Be Accountable.

The second area of strong concern communicated by various couples interviewed was being sure that you are called together. "There is a tendency not to listen to people and the concerns they express about your possibility of marrying someone of a different culture," one spouse said. "It's easy to begin thinking, 'It's us against them,' and close yourselves to some very valuable input, confrontation and honest hesitation provoked by these loved ones." In time, the goal can become a desire to beat the odds, prove the hesitant ones wrong and press on ignorantly in order to make your point. Decide to be very accountable to your pastor, your parents and to those relationships you value. Listen to them. Do not shut them out and react by drawing closer to your fiancé. Weigh their concerns and think through their questions.

Caution 3: Know What Both Cultures Value.

In North American culture, there is a tendency to value things. In many other countries the tendency is to value extended family, the elderly, hospitality—a "what's mine is yours" type of mentality. People become the primary concern; consequently, what people think of you is important. One husband mentioned that his culture is more formal and conservative, especially in dress. "My wife," he explained, "is much more casual. In my country I wear long-sleeved dress shirts. They must be clean and pressed or people will judge my spouse as a lazy wife."

One culture may value an education from the United States with such high regard that you would be expected to provide financially on a monthly basis for your extended family, as well as for others in need, after completing your education. Other cultures value spontaneity. In the European world, more information and a lot of clarity is valued.

North Americans tend to freely discuss their feelings and may take the liberty to share their negative feelings with you. Central Americans may hide their feelings, especially those of anger or conflict. They desire everything to appear fine between you and them. The traditional values in East Africa would expect that cooking and caring for the children is 100 percent the woman's job; the father may discipline the children, but not provide day-to-day care.

Caution 4: Identify Adaptation Versus Core Value Changes.

The final strong note of caution resulting from our survey concerned being aware of the difference between behavioral modification or adaptation and core value changes.

It is possible, for example, for a Middle Eastern man to adapt behaviorally to U.S. culture and look like he is, indeed, fitting into it. His core values may not have changed; he is simply conforming on the outside to the expectations of others. Because there is no inward change, this same man in his country of origin would look like, sound like and think like a Middle Easterner. Why? In his thinking he has not lied or deceived—just adapted. He can now be who he really is and perform according to what he has been taught by his family and culture. His unsuspecting wife finds herself living with a man whom she feels has made a radical about-face. She may feel trapped in a country and a culture with an unfamiliar person whom she thought she knew.

Accept and Appreciate Differences

Whether or not the values mentioned above are biblical is not the point, even though there will be times you may feel quite ready to argue that the way your culture did things is biblical. The point is that cultural differences exist, and you will be forced to face some of those mentioned and many that are not mentioned. If you choose to marry interculturally, you will need to learn to face cultural differences as a reality, not deny them.

Accepting and appreciating as many of the differences as you can will serve to enhance the marriage relationship. This experience is not to be viewed as all negative. The differences are something to embrace and value in one another. No two persons think alike or value the same things. You will need to give one another the freedom to be who you are and allow the Holy Spirit to mold the two cultures together. Rejoicing in the richness of your varied inheritances and learning from both is to be a joyous experience.

Homesickness

Realistically, no matter where you live, one of you will miss home. Understand that one or both of you will have parents who feel separated from their son or daughter and, someday, grandchildren.

Visits to the home country of one spouse can be very stressful. For example, there may be twenty-five or more relatives to visit within two short weeks! The foreign spouse may feel totally out of control of the situation. There is a larger than usual dependence on the "native" spouse to drive the car, do business at the bank and make decisions about other orders of business. The foreign spouse will need time to learn all of these things and will require many trips to become acclimated.

Also, the extended family will see the visiting spouse only in a vacation setting and not in a normal day-to-day lifestyle. This becomes an important area of communication for the couple, along with their families of origin.

Keep in mind that there can be a time frame of several years between visits with family members. Saying good-bye after your visit home or after your family visits you is a difficult, emotional challenge. Some individuals found the immediate time following a family visit was when they battled homesickness, and even depression, the most.

Be Sure!

In Exodus chapter 2, Moses was given a woman named Zipporah to marry. This marriage did not please all of Moses' family. Miriam and Aaron, Moses' sister and brother, began to speak against Moses, "because of his Cushite wife" (Numbers 12:1). There may be those, even within your own family, who would speak against an intercultural marriage. You must prepare yourself for this added pressure and/or rejection. Do your best not to respond negatively to this criticism. Not everyone will understand.

Ultimately, it is God who calls two people together—not diversity of culture or a common missionary spirit. One couple stated it so well: "Be absolutely, positively sure it is God and not infatuation, rebellion or some other emotion. Be in communication (with God and one another) at length, at all times and at all costs!" In addition to what this couple emphasized, be in communication with and receive counsel from your pastor and/or spiritual authority.

The following exercises will help you to think through your own assumptions or prejudices. Realize that if you haven't discussed these areas with your premarital counselors, it is imperative to do so.

Intercultural Marriages

Premarital Exercises

Intercultural Differences

Respond to each question or statement without the help of your fiancé. Be sure to express yourself clearly and thoroughly.

1. Where will you live when you are married? _____

   _____

   _____

2. If you are from different countries of origin, have you experienced living in each other's country? _____

   _____

   _____

3. After marriage, how often do you plan to return to your country of origin for visits (or your spouse's country if you will be living in your country of origin)? _____

   _____

   _____

4. Have you established peace with your parents in this decision? _____

   _____

   _____

   Discuss your parents' reactions, hesitations and encouragements.

   _____

   _____

   _____

5. Write about some cultural norms concerning male/female roles found within your country of origin. _____

_____

_____

6. What are some role differences that you notice now and know you will need to deal with in the future? _____

_____

_____

7. With two cultures merging into one, describe what steps you will take not to dictate your cultural norms to your spouse? _____

_____

_____

8. Describe how you hope your spouse will respond to you in terms of his/her cultural norms/expectations. _____

_____

_____

9. Have you discussed medical insurance and how it relates to the culture in which you plan to live? Have you shared your views on birth control with your future spouse? _____

_____

_____

Do ideas about birth control present possible conflict? Yes ____ No ____

10. In some countries, children born to parents of different races are called "half-castes." How will you deal with prejudice toward your children?

_____

_____

_____

11. Have you talked about where you want your children to be born?

_____

_____

_____

_____

Have you discussed how many children you desire to have?
Yes _____ No _____

12. Will your children be bilingual?   Yes _____ No _____

13. If the country you will live in offers a lower standard of education, where will your children be educated? _____

_____

_____

_____

14. During your engagement, how have you handled the challenges concerning intercultural marriage that you have received from others? _____

_____

_____

_____

Do you become defensive? Yes _____ No _____
Do you have a tendency to stick together and not deal with the challenge?
Yes _____ No _____

15. How have you demonstrated realism in addressing the differences that exist? _____

_____

_____

_____

16. Can you describe for yourself and for your spouse what you feel will be some of the losses that will need to be faced (for example, parents, family, conveniences, etc.)? _____

_____

_____

_____

How do you tend to respond to the emotions created by these losses?

_____

_____

_____

_____

17. While living in a foreign country, with whom will you be in close relationship other than your spouse? _____

_____

_____

18. Do you have any friends or relatives in the country where you are presently
living who can help hold you accountable through your engagement?
Yes _____ No _____

19. Once you are married, are there any couples whom you will be able to relate
to and pray with concerning future needs and differences that may arise?
Yes _____ No _____ If yes, who? _____

_____

20. Take time to write about attitudes concerning work and attitudes concerning leisure from your culture. How are they different than your
future spouse's? _____

_____

_____

_____

21. Will you need to learn another language? Yes _____ No _____
Are you willing to study another language? Yes _____ No _____

22. Will you need visas? Yes _____ No _____ Where are you in the
process of obtaining visas? _____

_____

Will this process require a time of physical separation following marriage?
Yes _____ No _____

23. Have you discussed medical care? _____

_____

What type of medical care is available in the country in which you will live?

_____

As compared to your country of origin, what are the differences in medical care? _____

_____

24. Have you discussed your parents' roles once you are married?
Yes _____ No _____
Are there any differences of opinion concerning your or your fiancé's parental involvement in your marriage? Yes _____ No _____
Have you discussed extended family roles and involvement/responsibilities?
Yes _____ No _____

25. Have you discovered any value differences concerning finances and budgeting?
Yes _____ No _____
Discuss any differences discovered. _____

_____

_____

_____

Have You Discussed?

Complete the following exercise separately by placing a check mark under yes, no or we need to discuss.

	Yes	No	Discuss
1. Food and meal preparation			
2. Home decorating			
3. Vacations as a couple and family			
4. The use of free time			
5. Celebration of important holidays			
6. Ways of educating children			
7. Dining out (how often/when)			
8. Spending money/allowance			
9. Spousal roles			
10. Ways of having fun			
11. Openness and the need for personal sharing			
12. Understanding of extended family			
13. Friendships within your fiancé's culture			
14. Spiritual differences			
15. Missing home			
16. Separation from family and friends			
17. Standard of living			
18. Facing prejudice			
19. Roles and discipline of children			
20. New and different ways of doing things			
21. Facing suspicion			
22. History of each other's culture			
23. Differing musical tastes			
24. Perceptions of time			
25. Political views and participation			
26. Your tendency to think your culture is "right"			
27. How you receive advice or counsel			

Scenario Communication

Please indicate how you will respond in the following situations.

1. You are not living in your country of origin. Your parents just left after a month-long visit. You feel like returning with them. How will you handle this emotional reaction? _____

    _____

    _____

    _____

    _____

2. You are pregnant with your first child and living away from your family of origin. You don't feel close to your in-laws who live in the same area as you do. How will you handle this problem? _____

    _____

    _____

    _____

    _____

3. You are living within your country of origin, which means your spouse is not. You begin to notice some depression in him/her and hear comments that would indicate homesickness. How will you help your spouse?

    _____

    _____

    _____

    _____

Intercultural Couple Dialogue

Find a couple who is interculturally married and ask them if they would be willing to communicate with you and your future spouse about some of the differences they have found. (Your pastor may be helpful in finding such a couple.) The following are suggested questions you can ask to generate dialogue between you as couples.

1. Could you share with us some of the positive experiences you have enjoyed as an intercultural marriage?
2. What are some of the negative experiences you've encountered?
3. Do you feel you've been able to uncover and deal with or replace the underlying assumption that my culture is "right"?
4. How does it feel for one of you to be living away from your family and country of origin?
5. How have you learned to appreciate the cultural differences?
6. What keeps your marriage strong in the midst of differences?
7. How do you prepare for and then handle visits to the home country of the spouse?
8. If one of you speaks a different language, how have you dealt with this?
9. What differences have you discovered concerning money and material things?
10. Can you share about your parents' involvement in your marriage?
11. What, if any, were areas of surprise to both of you?
12. If you met your spouse in your country of origin, can you discuss any differences you discovered in your spouse when living in or visiting his/her country of origin?

Personal Experience

As the two of you experience each other's country of origin and differences in culture before marriage, please discuss the positive and negative aspects of both.

1. When I experience my future spouse's culture, what I find to be positive is

   _____

   _____

   _____

   _____

2. What is negative for me is _____

   _____

   _____

   _____

3. Something I have difficulty understanding is _____

   _____

   _____

   _____

4. Some things that I saw as necessary for comfort in my country of origin that I will need to give up are _____

   _____

   _____

5. Something I've enjoyed learning about my future spouse's culture is

   _____

   _____

   _____

   _____

Intercultural Marriage

Postmarital Exercise

Postmarital Checkup for the Interculturally Married

Now that you are married, take the time to respond to each question or statement with the help of your spouse. A few of the questions may be more individual in nature.

1. What are some of the positive interculturally related experiences you as a couple have had since marriage? _____

   _____

   _____

2. What are some of the exciting things you have learned about an intercultural marriage? _____

   _____

   _____

3. Are there any negative experiences that you can share? _____

   _____

   _____

   _____

4. For the spouse who is living in a different country of origin, what are some of the surprise experiences you were unprepared for? _____

   _____

   _____

5. How are your parents feeling about your marriage at this point in time? Are you pleased with their amount of involvement in your marriage?

   _____

   _____

   _____

6. As you experience different cultural norms, how are you dealing with this?

   _____

   _____

   _____

7. How are you helping one another to adapt to an intercultural marriage?

_____

_____

8. Do you have any close relationships with individuals or other couples presently? Is there another couple or pastoral person to whom you as a couple are accountable? _____

_____

9. Have your different backgrounds helped you develop friendships where you are living? How have these different backgrounds made it more challenging to develop these friendships? _____

_____

10. Are either of you having to learn another language? If so, share your experience. _____

_____

11. Have you discovered a work ethic that differs from your country of origin's work ethic? _____

_____

12. Have you discussed your first visit to your partner's country of origin?

_____

_____

13. How can you be sensitive to your spouse when you are visiting your native country? _____

_____

14. Are there any significant food and meal preparation differences between you as a couple? _____

_____

15. What new or different ways of doing things have you discovered since marriage? _____

_____

16. Has there been any role confusion (due to differing beliefs) since your marriage? _____

_____

17. Have you discovered any cultural differences in the sexual realm of marriage? _____

_____

18. Have you as an intercultural couple faced any prejudice where you are presently living? _____

_____

19. In what ways are you having a tough time letting go of the idea that your way is right? How about your spouse? How do you think you can work further on this? _____

_____

20. Are there any other culturally related differences you have discovered? Please elaborate. _____

_____

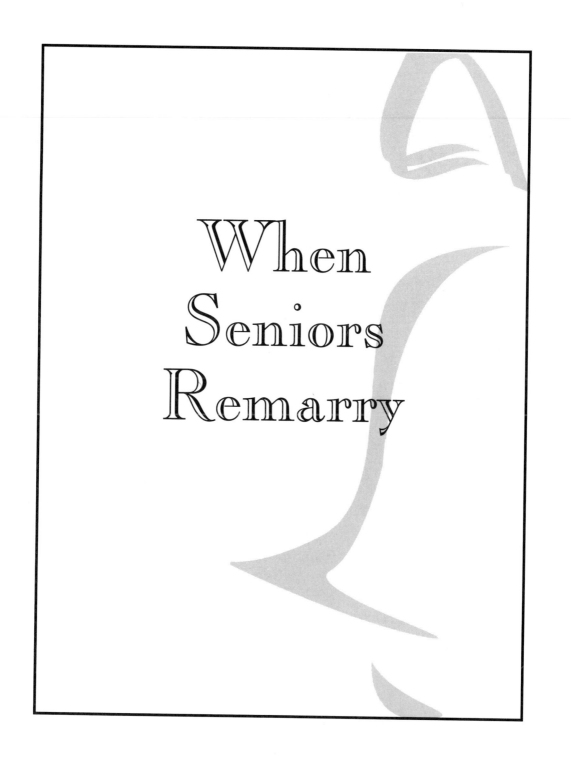

When Seniors Remarry

When Seniors Remarry

The fastest growing segment of population in the United States today is the group known as "senior citizens."

Most seniors expect to enjoy life during retirement from years of employment, to maintain reasonably good health and to have a lifelong partner at their sides. But what happens when that partner has preceded the other spouse to eternity? How does one deal with loneliness? Is it right to consider remarriage? Will the remaining spouse ever be happy again? Is it possible to feel excited about someone of the opposite sex and not feel guilty?

Sam and Helen had already experienced fifty-eight combined years of marriage before their spouses died. Helen said that people wanted her to get on with her life quickly. Comments like, "Isn't there anybody good enough for you?" only caused her to feel condemned, unable to meet the expectations of those around her. Helen eventually sold her home and moved in with her son and daughter-in-law.

Meanwhile, in a neighboring town, Sam was allowing one of his four adult daughters to move into his home with her new husband. "We can help you, Dad, with the loss of Mom," they said, "and pay you rent."

When Sam and Helen were able to move on from their grief and loss, they found each other. Both were finishing up teaching careers and neither of them had been desirous of joining the "dating scene." Although both knew the pain of loneliness, neither Sam nor Helen were willing to consider remarriage. Armed with their strong faith, Sam and Helen both depended on God to meet their emotional needs. But God chose to meet those needs by bringing them together in marriage.

Today, at the age of sixty-four, after eight years of marriage, they are no longer lonely and rejoice that they could find happiness and fulfillment in a new spouse.

What were some of the obstacles along the way for this precious couple? Before you work through the questions in the exercises that follow, let us give you some background through the lives of Sam and Helen. Perhaps you'll be able to identify with some of their thoughts.

Losses

Sam and Helen illustrate some of the losses that are encountered when walking through the bereavement of a spouse. The intimacy one has had with a life-long partner is beyond description. So much in this area can be taken for granted (for example, sharing secrets, having a deep familiarization with one person, the small acts of service, the security represented by this partner, personal gifts, powerful and meaningful words stated too infrequently and just having someone at your side).

The above thoughts can perhaps be summed up in one word. That word is *companionship*. Webster calls it a "matched pair or set." The loss of companionship affects us more deeply than the loss of financial resources or anything material. Jesus referred to the deep void one feels in lost companionship when He cried out from the cross, "My God, my God, why have you forsaken me?" (Mark 15:34).

Have you effectively worked through your losses? Do you still hurt, or are you angry at God, others or yourself? Do you feel any guilt from your former marriage? Ask Jesus about these things and then ask Him for healing.

Adult Children

Sam and Helen knew their relationship would mean adjustments when relating to their grown children. Even though the children said that they were "all for" their parents' newfound love relationship, many changes would be forthcoming.

After the loss of one parent, an adult child can have difficulty seeing his/her mother or father grow close to someone of the opposite sex. The parent desires to share his/her feelings of excitement with the children, but is not sure if they want to hear about them. Helen said that it is "kind of a role reversal. Your children ask if you have held hands yet or if you have kissed. It is uncomfortable for them." In one sense, they want to know in order to share their parent's joy. In another sense, however, they would rather not know the details.

One daughter felt like her father was moving too quickly. Sam and Helen's response was, "Why prolong the process? We both knew what we wanted and felt God's blessing upon our desires."

Another area to be dealt with was that of family heirlooms. Sam gave all of his former wife's heirlooms to his daughters. "After all," Sam said, "Helen and I didn't need them and this way they needed to have no fear that they wouldn't receive these items in the future."

An adjustment in relationships will also be necessary. When Helen decided to remarry, the son with whom she was living began to experience feelings of loss—Mom would no longer live in his home. Helen and her daughter-in-law were very close; the living arrangement prior to remarriage had worked well. Her daughter-in-law said, "I feel like I'm losing my best friend."

Finances

Sam and Helen have financial advice for those who are remarrying: Be open and honest from the beginning. Do not separate finances, but bring them together. In order to have this union succeed, a couple needs to have financial unity and move away from a "his and hers" mentality.

Some seniors are choosing to live together and remain unmarried solely based upon financial reasons. These persons do not desire to alter their retirement benefits or Social Security status. Even if a couple claims a platonic relationship, the appearance is a concern. Listen to the following verses found in First Thessalonians 5:21-22: "Test everything. Hold on to the good. Avoid every kind of evil." (Or "the appearance of evil," some texts read.) We are admonished to avoid anything that is questionable or could be seen as wrongdoing.

As well, First Timothy 6:10 informs us, "Some people, eager for money, have wandered from the faith and pierced themselves with many griefs." While you may not be "eager for money," basing your decision on financial income rather than faith in God's ability to supply all of our needs (Philippians 4:11-13, 19) is an act of trusting self more than God. God is a better provider than the government or any retirement plan.

Sharing Memories

Sam and Helen recommend to seniors who are serious about remarriage that they talk about their former spouses during their first weeks of courting.

"We spent a lot of time sharing about our first love," Helen said.

It was not conversation full of comparison, Sam said, just "letting it all out with someone who understood the experience."

"We recognized that when we shared all that we needed to share," Helen said, "we could then move on to other important areas of getting to know one another."

Sam and Helen made a promise to one another that they would not be involved in comparison during their courtship or throughout their marriage. They have maintained this promise.

As you work through the exercises that follow, allow the Holy Spirit to point out and impress within you any areas where there is still confusion, hurt, loneliness or loss. Our Father is a Redeemer. Be open for prayer and input from your premarital counselors.

Loneliness

1. Describe the difference between "aloneness" and "loneliness." _____
   _____
   _____

   How have you experienced both of these? _____
   _____

2. Where is God when one is experiencing loneliness? _____
   _____

3. Describe the benefits of loneliness. _____
   _____

4. How can loneliness serve as a life discipline? _____
   _____

5. What have you discovered about yourself in loneliness? _____
   _____

6. Does your "single identity" leave you feeling lonely? Please expound.
   _____
   _____

7. How does Psalm 139:1-12 speak to your loneliness? _____
   _____

8. Are you considering marriage as an escape from loneliness? _____
   _____

Scenarios

1. Within the first year of remarriage, your new partner suffers a debilitating stroke. How will you handle this unexpected condition? _____

_____

_____

_____

2. Two years into your new marriage, certain family members are still "horrified" that you would remarry. How will you confront this disappointment?

_____

_____

_____

_____

_____

3. You can't help but feel as though your new husband/wife has a strong desire to have you be like his/her former spouse. Since this is not your goal, what will you do? _____

_____

_____

_____

4. Keeping in contact with two families has become increasingly difficult. What steps can you take to remedy the situation? _____

_____

_____

_____

Other Questions to Consider

1. Some adult children feel their dad or mom have the courtship in "over-drive." Have any of your children expressed this? Yes _____ No _____

2. Do your adult children desire to hear about your dates or do they avoid the subject? _____

   _____

   _____

3. Have you discovered any form of "role reversal" with your adult children? In other words, are they "checking up" on you and your fiancé's relationship? If so, has this been a problem or a blessing? _____

   _____

   _____

   _____

4. What do you desire your step-grandchildren to call you? _____

   _____

   _____

   _____

   _____

5. Have you discussed family heirlooms? Do you both keep, sell or give away family heirlooms? _____

   _____

   _____

   _____

6. There can be a loyalty issue with possessions like furniture. Have you taken the time to discuss personal possessions? If so, what have you decided?

   _____

   _____

   _____

7. There are aspects of life that are "set in concrete." What are some of the areas you consider nonnegotiable? _____

_____

_____

8. How will you leave independence and create a spirit of interdependence?

_____

_____

_____

9. What church will you attend? _____

_____

_____

10. Where will you live? _____

_____

_____

11. How will you handle your savings accounts, retirement accounts and any indebtedness? _____

_____

_____

12. Where does your pastor and/or spiritual leader(s) stand as you consider remarriage? _____

_____

_____

13. Are your parents still living?   Yes _____ No _____ Have they given you any advice concerning remarriage? _____

_____

_____

14. How long have you lived without a life partner? What do you foresee as your most difficult adjustment? _____

_____

_____

15. When seniors consider remarriage, sometimes dreams about their departed life partners increase. How will you deal with this? _____

_____

_____

16. As you consider spousal roles once again, what previous roles did you play that you do not wish to repeat in a new marriage? _____

_____

_____

17. Did you have any expectations that were not fulfilled in your first marriage? Yes _____ No _____ What were they? _____

_____

_____

18. What good thing(s) from your previous marriage do you desire to bring into this new union? _____

_____

_____

19. If you are presently living in a retirement home, have you researched their policies on residents and marriage? _____

_____

_____

_____

20. What will you gain by going from dating to marriage? _____
_____
_____
_____
_____

What are some possible losses? _____
_____
_____
_____

21. Have you discussed wedding plans?   Yes _____ No _____
How do they differ from first-time weddings? _____
_____

22. Have you discussed sexual attraction?   Yes _____ No _____
What part will sex play in your marriage? _____
_____

What about sexual impotency?   Yes _____ No _____
23. What fears, if any, are you feeling about remarriage? _____
_____
_____
_____

24. Are you presently experiencing any feelings of disloyalty to your former
spouse? Yes _____ No _____ If yes, please expound.
_____
_____
_____

25. Have you effectively worked through your loss of a life partner? Some of those losses include: deep familiarization with another, oneness and losing mutual friendships, losing a parent of your children and the loss of finances. _____

_____

_____

_____

_____

Appendices

Appendix A

Are You on Schedule?

Check this wedding timetable.
- Discuss possible engagement with parents. Be sure of their approval.
- Discuss possible engagement with those in spiritual authority (pastor, associate pastor, premarital counselor, etc.).
- Seek counsel concerning an appropriate time frame for the wedding.

The Bride's Timetable
Six Months to a Year before the Wedding

1. Discuss and set wedding budget with parents. Include groom and his parents in discussions if they are sharing costs.
2. Review, evaluate and comparison shop for wedding sites. Select a wedding date, time and place as soon as possible.
3. Start making guest list.
4. Plan color scheme for ceremony and reception.
5. Select and order wedding dress.
6. Choose attendants for wedding and invite them to participate.
7. Reserve caterer and musicians.
8. Register at one or more stores for china, silverware and other household items.
9. Purchase wedding ring for groom.

Three Months before the Wedding

1. Complete guest lists and check for duplication.
2. Order invitations, enclosure cards and personal stationery (for thank-you notes and future use).
3. Address invitations.
4. Choose wedding party attire for bridesmaids' dresses and mothers of bride and groom. Groom and male attendants should select outfits.

5. Shop for trousseau.
6. Hire photographer and/or videographer to record wedding day.
7. Arrange for bridal portrait, if being taken ahead of time.
8. Arrange for tests for marriage license, if required.
9. Discuss ceremony and music with appropriate personnel.
10. Finalize reception plans.
11. Order wedding cake.
12. Order wedding flowers for bridal party, ceremony and reception.
13. Mail invitations.

One Month before the Wedding

1. Check guidelines for newspaper wedding announcements. Prepare the announcement and send in when required.
2. Have final dress fitting.
3. Have wedding portrait taken.
4. Choose and order gifts for attendants.
5. Select gift for groom.
6. Arrange accommodations for out-of-town relatives and attendants.
7. Plan bridesmaids' party, if giving one.

Three Weeks before the Wedding

1. Get marriage license with fiancé.
2. Arrange transportation for bridal party to ceremony.
3. Discuss details of wedding and reception with photographer (or videographer).
4. Remind each member of the wedding party of the date, time and place of rehearsal and wedding.

One Week before the Wedding

1. Begin honeymoon packing.
2. Give or go to the bridesmaids' party; present gifts to attendants at bridesmaids' party or rehearsal dinner.
3. Provide final estimate of number of reception guests to caterer.
4. Check on final details with florist, photographer and musicians.
5. Arrange to move wedding gifts and personal belongings to your new home.

The Groom's Timetable

Six Months before the Wedding

1. Order engagement and wedding rings for the bride.
2. Start guest list.
3. Select best man and other attendants (usually one usher for each fifty guests).
4. Discuss honeymoon plans with bride and begin making arrangements.

Three Months before the Wedding

1. Complete guest list; make sure addresses are correct.
2. Consult with bride about appropriate dress for you and male attendants.
3. Complete honeymoon plans and purchase tickets.
4. Consult with bride on flowers for bridal bouquet and going-away corsage (usually paid for by groom).
5. Arrange accommodations for out-of-town relatives and ushers.

One Month before the Wedding

1. Pick up wedding rings; check on engraving.
2. Help plan rehearsal dinner if your parents are hosting.
3. Select gift for bride.
4. Choose gifts for attendants. Make sure documents are in order (legal, medical and religious).

Three Weeks before the Wedding

1. Get marriage license.
2. Check on arrangements for bachelor dinner if you are giving one.
3. Arrange for transportation to and from reception site.

One Week before the Wedding

1. Remind best man and ushers of rehearsal time and place.
2. Present gifts to attendants.
3. Explain any special seating needs to head usher.
4. Get wedding clothes and going-away clothes ready.

Appendix B

Who Pays for What?

The following are general guidelines and not to be taken legalistically.

Bride

1. Wedding ring for the groom
2. A wedding gift for the groom
3. Gifts for the bridal attendants
4. Personal stationery
5. Medical examination and blood test
6. Accommodations for out-of-town attendants

Groom

1. The bride's engagement and wedding rings
2. A wedding gift for the bride
3. Gifts for the best man and ushers
4. Groom's wedding attire
5. Bride's bouquet and going-away corsage
6. Mothers' corsages
7. Boutonnieres for attendants and fathers
8. Medical examination and blood test
9. Marriage license
10. Clergyman's fee
11. Honeymoon expenses
12. Bachelor dinner (if not given by the best man, optional)

Bride's family

1. Engagement party (optional)
2. Ceremony cost: location, music, rentals and all related expenses

3. Entire cost of reception: food, beverages, entertainment, rental items, decorations, wedding cake
4. Bride's wedding attire and accessories
5. Wedding gift for the couple
6. Wedding invitations, announcements and mailing costs
7. Bridesmaids' bouquets
8. Transportation for bridal party from bride's home to the site of ceremony
9. Bridesmaids' luncheon
10. Photography (groom's parents may pay for the pictures they would like)
11. Personal wedding attire
12. Floral decorations

Groom's family

1. Rehearsal dinner party
2. Personal wedding attire
3. Travel and accommodations for groom's family
4. Wedding gift for the couple
5. Special items they may wish to purchase: toasting goblets, ring pillow, etc.
6. Any general expenses they may wish to contribute to

Appendix C

Birth Control

Children are a unique gift from God and provide a lifetime of blessing. The psalmist said, "Sons are a heritage from the LORD, children a reward from him. . . . Blessed is the man whose quiver is full of them" (127:3, 5). God has given us the ability to combine genes and see another human being with certain traits come forth. This "child" is the "heritage" that provides the "reward" of blessing to this new union.

God encouraged us in Genesis 1:28 to "be fruitful and increase in number; fill the earth." Therefore, marriage includes procreation. Some teach that a "quiver" contained five arrows. God leaves the decision concerning the number of children you give birth to up to you. Most Christians use some method of birth control, so we include a section on the subject. Each couple should pray and agree concerning the number of children they can train to serve God.

The following information was written by Scott Jackson, M.D. It is not all-inclusive but does provide a concise look at several methods of birth control. As a couple, pray, consult your physician and educate yourselves. There are certain types of oral contraceptives which would be considered abortive. You may want to ask your doctor directly, "Is this method of birth control abortive?"

Again, we recommend that you discuss this important matter with your family physician or contact the National Right to Life, Suite 402, 4197th Street N.W., Washington, DC 20004; telephone 202-626-8800 with any questions.

Options

Oral Contraceptives

Ovulation is directed by hormones, mainly estrogen and progesterone. Oral contraceptives consist of man-made versions of these hormones. They work to prevent the ovaries from producing eggs. Also, they help prevent sperm from reaching an egg. Several types of oral contraceptives exist with different levels of hormones. They also are available in twenty-one-day or twenty-eight-day packs. Your doctor can determine which is right for you. Oral contraceptives are the most effective birth control method. Side effects are rare but can include headaches, weight gain, breast tenderness and midcycle bleeding. There is a higher chance of blood clots or vascular disease, especially if one smokes, while on the pill. The use of oral contraceptives must be monitored by a physician and must include yearly pap tests.

Diaphragm

The diaphragm is a soft rubber or latex cup that is inserted into the vagina to cover the cervix. It works as a barrier to sperm and is used with spermicidal jelly or cream, which kills sperm before they enter the uterus and fertilize the egg. The diaphragm will need to be fitted by your physician. He will instruct you on how to insert it and how to apply the spermicide. The diaphragm is highly effective if properly used. It must be inserted prior to intercourse each time. Afterward, it can be cleaned with soap and water. The diaphragm should be replaced every two years.

Spermicides

Spermicides kill sperm so none can enter the uterus and fertilize an egg. They consist of jellies, cream, foam or suppositories. When used with a diaphragm, they can be highly effective. Some use foam or suppositories without a diaphragm. They can be obtained without a prescription and are rather inexpensive. However, their effectiveness as birth control is not as high as the two previous methods mentioned.

Cervical Cap

The cervical cap is a smaller version of the diaphragm. It consists of a slightly thicker rubber and is filled with spermicidal jelly or cream. It should be fitted by your physician and must be rechecked yearly. The cervical cap is applied at the time of each intercourse.

Condoms

The condom is a thin shield of latex that fits over the man's penis. It traps expelled semen during intercourse, preventing sperm from fertilizing an egg. The condom should be applied to the erect penis before intercourse. Afterward, the man should withdraw immediately to prevent leakage. Condoms should be used in combination with spermicidal suppositories, jelly, cream or foam as a backup form of birth control in case of leakage or breakage. Condoms, in general, are not as effective in birth control as the pill or diaphragm.

Contraceptive Sponges

The contraceptive sponge is a small, disposable, round, spermicide-containing sponge, which can be purchased over-the-counter. Use of the sponge can be fairly expensive because a new sponge must be used each time a couple has intercourse. Water is applied to the sponge, and it is inserted over the cervix. It does provide twenty-four-hour protection and is about as effective as the diaphragm, except in women who have already had children.

Natural Family Planning

Natural family planning utilizes the fact that fertilization is most likely to occur just before, during or after ovulation. It is the least effective birth control method since even the most regular cycles can vary from month to month. The woman can monitor her ovulation schedule by checking her body temperature every morning and plotting it on a calendar for several months. She usually sees a slight rise in temperature during ovulation. Usually a pattern occurs, alerting the couple to avoid intercourse during the most fertile days. Most find that ovulation occurs fourteen days before the start of the next menstrual period. Another way of determining ovulation is cervical mucus charting which involves observing a sample of mucus from the vagina daily. The mucus becomes clear, elastic and slippery during ovulation.

Appendix D

Honeymoon Precautions

Sometimes new brides, especially those who are virgins, develop some painful, if not embarrassing, symptoms during or shortly after the honeymoon. We have included short descriptions of "honeymoon cystitis" and vaginitis as preventative information for the new bride and groom.

Cystitis

The urethra or tube draining urine from the bladder can be easily bruised, especially if not enough lubrication is provided for the penis to be inserted into the vagina. "Honeymoon cystitis" can result in bladder pain, bloody urine or burning upon urination. Bruising of the urethra allows bacteria to grow in the urine stream causing an infection. This can easily be cured with antibiotic therapy and by drinking plenty of fluids. Repeated attacks can sometimes be prevented by urinating after each time of intercourse.

Vaginitis

Vaginitis, inflammation of the vagina, may have a host of causes. Usually, the woman will experience burning or unusual vaginal discharge. Sometimes painful intercourse results. She should seek medical attention in the event of any suspicion of vaginitis. There are over-the-counter preparations which promote effective cures; however, these should be used only under the recommendations of a physician. Some types of vaginitis can be passed from wife to husband and may require antibiotics for both partners.

Appendix E

Answer Key

Matching Questions

1. T
2. Z
3. P
4. J
5. D
6. C
7. Y
8. H
9. N
10. L
11. B
12. R
13. F
14. W
15. A
16. M
17. I
18. E
19. Q
20. K
21. U
22. S
23. V
24. X
25. O
26. G

Anatomy Questions

Male

8. glans penis
3. penis
4. prostate gland
2. scrotum
7. seminal vesicles
1. testicle
5. urethra
6. vas deferens

Female

1. cervix
7. clitoris
4. fallopian tube
6. labia
3. ovary
8. urethra
5. uterus or womb
2. vagina

True or False Questions

1. T
2. T
3. F
4. T
5. T
6. F
7. T
8. T
9. T
10. F
11. T
12. T
13. T
14. T
15. T
16. F
17. T
18. F
19. T
20. F

Appendix F

Resource List

Additional books for instruction and reading pleasure recommended by the authors:

Backus, Dr. William. *Telling Yourself the Truth*. Minneapolis, MN: Bethany House Publishers, 1980.

Burkett, Larry. *Answers to Your Family's Financial Questions*. Pomona, CA: Focus on the Family, 1987.

Cole, Edwin Louis. *Maximized Manhood*. Springdale, PA: Whitaker House, 1982.

Crabb, Dr. Larry. *The Marriage Builder: A Blueprint for Couples and Counselors*. Grand Rapids, MI: Pyranee Books, 1982.

Dobson, Dr. James. *Love for a Lifetime*. Sisters, OR: Multnomah Books, 1996.

Exley, Richard. *The Rhythm of Life: Putting Life's Priorities in Perspective*. Tulsa, OK: Honor Books, 1987.

Hart, Archibald. *The Sexual Man*. Dallas, TX: Word, Inc., 1994.

Hart, Archibald, Catherine Weber and Debra Taylor. *The Secrets of Eve*. Dallas, TX: Word, Inc., 1998.

Hunt, Art. *Praying with the One You Love*. Sisters, OR: Multnomah Books, 1996.

McManus, Michael. *Marriage Savers: Helping Your Friends and Family Avoid Divorce*. Grand Rapids, MI: Zondervan Publishing House, 1993.

Parrot, Les and Leslie. *Becoming Soul Mates*. Grand Rapids, MI: Zondervan Publishing House, 1995.

_____. *Questions Couples Ask*. Grand Rapids, MI: Zondervan Publishing House, 1996.

Rainey, Dennis and Barbara. *Moments Together for Couples*. Ventura, CA: Regal Books, 1995.

Roberts, Lee. *Praying God's Will for My Marriage*. Nashville, TN: Thomas Nelson Publishers, 1994.

Seamonds, David A. *Healing for Damaged Emotions: Recovering from Memories That Cause Pain*. Wheaton, IL: Victor Books, 1981.

Smalley, Gary. *If Only He Knew: A Valuable Guide to Knowing, Understanding and Loving Your Wife*. Grand Rapids, MI: Pyranee Books, 1988.

_____. *Love Is a Decision: Ten Proven Principles to Energize Your Marriage and Family*. Dallas, TX: Word Publishing, 1989.

Wheat, Ed, M.D. *Intended for Pleasure: Sexual Technique and Sexual Fulfillment in Marriage*. Old Tappan, NJ: Fleming H. Revell Co., 1977.

_____. *Love Life for Every Married Couple*. Grand Rapids, MI: Pyranee Books, 1980.

Williams, Pat and Jill. *Keep the Fire Glowing: How a Loving Marriage Builds a Loving Family*. Old Tappan, NJ: Fleming H. Revell Co., 1986.

Wright, H. Norman. *Understanding the Man in Your Life*. Dallas, TX: Word Publishing, 1987.

Counselor's Guide

Counselor's Guide

Where can an engaged couple find clear, biblical premarital instruction? Did you and your spouse participate in any type of premarital counseling? We encourage you to take time to answer the following questions:

1. Did you and your spouse receive premarital counseling?
   Yes _____ No _____
2. Did your pastor require that you have premarital counseling?
   Yes _____ No _____
3. Who administered your premarital counseling? _____
4. How many sessions of counseling did you attend? _____
5. What were the topics discussed in each session? _____

   _____

   _____

6. Did you receive any homework assignments? Yes _____ No _____
   Did you complete the assignments? Yes _____ No _____
7. Were you assigned any books to read? Yes _____ No _____
   If yes, what were the titles of the books? _____

   _____

   _____

8. Did you complete any personality assessments or other tests?
   Yes _____ No _____
9. Was the sexual relationship discussed to your satisfaction?
   Yes _____ No _____
10. Were finances discussed in detail? Yes _____ No _____
11. Rate your premarital counseling. (1 = inadequate, 10 = excellent)_____
12. How much effect did your premarital counseling have upon your marriage relationship? (1 = very little; 10 = very much)_____
13. Did you receive any postmarital counseling? Yes _____ No _____

While training local church couples to give premarital counseling, we asked some of these same questions. Many couples struggled to remember whether or not they had participated in premarital counseling. Some couples could not remember what content had been covered in their counseling.

One couple shared that they met with a psychologist for two premarital sessions. When asked why they attended only two sessions, they replied, "That's all we could afford." This is a sad testimony to where the church has been in relation to training couples for marriage.

Where does a couple go for marriage training? The answer is obvious: to the church. Most couples desire to have a church wedding. However, many pastors have shied away from in-depth premarital counseling sessions for several reasons. One reason is the time commitment involved. Most pastors have tight schedules. Sadly, a second reason is the lack of comprehensive materials available to pastors.

Another question for pastors to consider is this: What is your philosophy concerning premarital education? Your philosophy will determine your premarital counseling process and the type of curriculum you use.

Called Together is unique in that it is administered couple-to-couple. We have successfully trained committed Christian couples rather than busy pastors to administer the pre- and postmarital instruction. They have committed themselves to work with a premarital couple for six or more sessions. This time frame allows for a quality relationship to develop, which continues through the postmarital sessions. Couples who want to be married at our church are required to participate in premarital counseling. Throughout the counseling process, they are challenged and encouraged. As the counselor couple studies the premarital material, they also become vulnerable and accountable to the couple whom they are counseling.

Let us share some reasons why we believe pre- and postmarital counseling is extremely important:

- Marriage was designed by God. We need to do our best to see each marriage built upon a proper foundation.
- Premarital counseling will expose potential problem areas. As these problem areas are exposed, they can be lovingly dealt with. This is preventative counseling at its best.
- Premarital counseling will build the faith of the couple or it will reveal to the couple that they are, in fact, not called together. *Note:* We do not refuse

premarital counseling to anyone. However, we also make no promises to marry anyone. What we do, we must do in faith (Romans 14:23).

- Premarital counseling can be provocative and challenging.
- Premarital counseling helps the couple to get their heads "out of the clouds," to face differences and reality.
- Postmarital counseling is a checkup and review, their first oil change, so to speak. Postmarital counseling within the first year of marriage provides opportunities for guidance, feedback and prayer and nurtures a healthy environment in which to discuss troublesome areas of the marriage.
- Postmarital counseling reflects reality now that the couple has said, "I do." They now "know" one another. Faults and weaknesses have been exposed. The counseling couple can affirm strengths and encourage growth.

If we believe in strong, Christ-centered families, we must believe in and institute a thorough pre- and postmarital program.

This manual is a guide to the effective use of the *Called Together* pre- and postmarital program. *Called Together* is designed to provoke the couple to think and respond in writing. Each session will be approximately two hours long. Confidentiality on the part of both couples is essential. Disclosure is vital and details should not be discussed outside of the counseling sessions without permission.

Counselor couples must be willing to share about their marriage and provide a godly role model. They must also be willing to talk about difficult areas with the marriage relationship. They cannot be embarrassed to discuss such topics as childhood, family of origin issues, sexual foreplay, salvation and so forth. Counselor couples need to be able to ask pertinent questions. Dependence upon the Spirit of God is essential. The Holy Spirit can reveal hidden areas such as family curses; previous sexual involvement; past physical, emotional or sexual abuse; unhealthy relationships from the counselee's past. Counselor couples must not be afraid to confront sin in a loving manner.

The remainder of this instructional notebook will provide specific directions for each counseling session. Personalize each session according to the particular couple's needs. Pray with the couple frequently. Be sure to maintain accountability in all areas, with special focus on the couple's physical relationship while they are engaged.

God bless you as you provide thorough pre- and postmarital counseling to better equip the saints.

Counselor's Guide to

Premarital Sessions

Before Premarital Session One

The following instructions will help you to initiate the premarital training efficiently and with confidence. *Called Together* is best administered couple-to-couple. Consequently, a relationship will develop that could carry on throughout the new marriage. Before Session One, the engaged couple should receive the *Called Together* manuals and complete the Identification Data (found on pages xviii-xxi), as well as the first six homework exercises ("About Me," "Spiritual Overview," "Individual Mission," "Biblical Concept of Love," "Sexual Boundaries," "Who I Am in Christ").

We recommend the FOCCUS (Facilitating Open Couple Communication, Understanding and Study) inventory for the couples you will be taking through premarital counseling. This instrument for marriage preparation can be ordered with an eighty-five page facilitator's manual, which introduces and walks you through use of the tool.

Couples are given a 156-question list with additional questions for interfaith marriage, second marriage and cohabiting couples. You can order a Christian nondenominational, Spanish, Alternate (learning disability) or Catholic edition. A ReFocus edition for couples considering remarriage is also available.

For more information or to order contact Family Life Office, 3214 North 60th Street, Omaha, NE 68104-3495 or call 402-551-9003.

Important: All of these assignments are to be completed and turned in to you, the counselor, *before* Session One. This will facilitate your review of their recorded answers and help prepare you to personalize the counseling sessions according to their needs as a couple. Assignments for the remaining sessions should also be completed and in your possession *before* the corresponding session.

It may be advisable to meet with the couple before initiating any premarital sessions. During this time you should assess their relationship with God and whether or not God is calling you to be involved in their premarital training. For those who are equipped not only to give premarital training, but also to perform the actual marriage ceremony, it would be advisable to tell the couple that being involved in premarital counseling is no guarantee that you will perform the wedding ceremony. Performing the actual ceremony is something that God must give you faith for only after He has confirmed the couple and their call together.

Should you agree to counsel the couple, you will have one session for each of the six major sections of the manual. We recommend giving copies of the books *Love Life for Every Married Couple* by Ed Wheat and *Maximized Manhood* by Edwin Louis Cole to the couple at the beginning of the premarital counseling. A copy of the book *The Act of Marriage* by Tim and Beverly LaHaye can be given when you sense it is appropriate for the couple to begin reading about sexual relations. The books should be read by the counselees before the last session of counseling. (Again, an exception may be *The Act of Marriage*. Some couples have expressed difficulty with their physical relationship due to the explicit nature of the material covered in this book.)

In Appendix A and Appendix B you will find helpful resources for the couple to use in the planning stage of the wedding. Birth control information is available in Appendix C, and Appendix D offers honeymoon precautions.

Called Together
Premarital Course Overview

Introduction to the Premarital Course

A. Goals of Premarital Training:

1. To introduce the couple to God's institution of marriage
2. To thoroughly prepare a couple for marriage

B. Sub-goals of Premarital Training:

1. To assist the couple in taking an honest look at themselves
2. To help the couple in evaluating their present relationship
3. To improve communication skills
4. To aid in the development of financial skills and financial accountability
5. To provide accurate and appropriate information in the area of sexual relations
6. To aid the couple in ceremony planning

C. Objectives of Premarital Training will be met:

1. By attending at least five premarital sessions and one marriage ceremony planning session
2. By studying scriptural marriage concepts
3. By observing aspects of marriage exemplified by couple counselors
4. By completing reading and writing assignments
5. By completing a relationship profile and the FOCCUS inventory
6. By participating in open discussion, Bible study and prayer

About Me

Premarital Session One

In order to prepare couples for a God-honoring and personally satisfying relationship in marriage, an initial marital readiness assessment should be conducted. To assist the counselor, spiritual overviews of both individuals and "About Me" work sheets are included in the assignments for Session One. Discuss the intent of these work sheets in Session One in order to help determine potential spiritual conflict or compatibility. Responses to the "About Me" questions will reveal a wealth of individual reactions to anger, fear, guilt and so forth. Realistically speaking, a person never sees beyond the "nice" side of his/her fiancé. He or she will not be prepared to face difficulties or conflicts in marriage unless he or she sees the "other" side.

Session One is the time to administer the Relationship Profile or a personality tool which you have been trained to use. For more information on the Relationship Profile, you may write or call the authors of *Called Together*. You may give the results to the couple in Session Two or throughout the premarital sessions. However you choose to use this tool, be considerate and wise when revealing the information to the couple.

A scriptural review of love should be included in Session One. The exercise "A Biblical Concept of Love" offers a basis for this discussion. Wedding timetables found in Appendix A are included to assist the couple in making plans for their wedding, and a handout entitled "Who Pays for What?" (Appendix B, pg. 210) will help clarify financial obligations.

It will be important as counselors to address the individual responses to the exercise "Individual Mission." Frequently, singles make marriage their goal. Marriage is not the goal, but rather, seeing the individual call of God in their lives joined to become a cooperative mission. Are their individual missions compatible or are they too diverse to be united? An example of diverse missions could be the following: Don senses a strong call of God to minister to inner-city youth while Beth, having participated in several short-term mission trips, feels a strong leading toward foreign missions. Are these missions compatible? Can they become compatible?

The mission exercises in chapters one and two will help you, as counselors, and the engaged couple to assess the plausibility of the prospective marriage mission.

Remember, do not make any assumptions concerning this couple. Treat them as if they know nothing about marriage preparation even if one or both have been previously married.

For a spiritual overview, you will want to discuss the following topics and Scriptures:

Salvation . . . . John 3:3; Romans 10:9
Sin. . . . . Romans 3:10, 23
Lordship . . . . Luke 14:33
Water Baptism . . . . Matthew 28:19; Acts 16:33
The Holy Spirit . . . . Matthew 3:11; Acts 1:8
Prayer. . . . . Luke 18:1; 1 Thessalonians 5:17
The Word. . . . . Psalm 119:11, 105; Ephesians 6:17; Hebrews 4:12
Church Attendance. . . . . Hebrews 10:25

Finally, discuss purity with the couple. Consider these four areas:

1. Seek God first (Matthew 6:33).
2. Commit yourselves to purity (1 Timothy 5:1-2).
3. Be committed to communication so as to not defraud one another (Ephesians 4:15).
4. Be committed to accountability with parents, pastor and counselors (Luke 16:1-15).

About Us

Premarital Session Two

Many couples enter marriage unrealistically. God wants us to be full of faith but "wise as serpents." With the great wealth of literature, videos and audio tapes available on the subjects of marriage, sex, finances, communication and so forth, no couple should enter marriage unaware of Satan's devices to undermine and destroy relationships.

Reasons for marriage can vary widely. The exercises "Reasons for Marriage" and "Expectations and Perceptions of Marriage" help the counselor and the couple to sift through the emotional and romantic issues to determine the valid call of God to marriage.

Is this couple compatible in the expectations and perceptions of marriage? Potential areas of conflict could be identified as you review both sets of expectations in your counseling session. Be careful not only to point out potential problem areas, but also the positives from areas of agreement. Point the couple to Scripture passages that provide answers for the possible conflicts.

Normally, engaged couples will have the following three expectations:

1. They expect that this marriage will never end in divorce.
2. They expect faithfulness and commitment from each other.
3. They expect minimal adjustments and few, if any, problems.

Be aware that when expectations are not met they can become demands. Please share some of your premarital and postmarital expectations that were not met by your partner and how you dealt with these unmet expectations.

The exercise on reactions deals with "what if" situations. Hopefully the couple will not have to face any of these situations. But what if . . . ? Use God's Word to address these situations, offering God's hope for any problem that could arise.

The following exercise provokes discussion about parents. Family of origin issues are an essential topic for premarital counseling. Does the couple have their parents' blessing? Take the time to discuss this exercise. But be aware that these questions cannot possibly cover every issue that pertains to the family of origin.

Cover the exercise "Are You Ready to Leave and Cleave?" thoroughly with the engaged couple.

Let's Talk

Premarital Session Three

Effective communication is vital to a stable, intimate and satisfying marriage relationship. A breakdown of communication is almost always a primary cause of marital dysfunction. Ed Cole, in his book *Communication, Sex and Money*, states that when communication stops, abnormality sets in, and the ultimate end of abnormality is death of the relationship. Just as faith dies when we refuse to communicate with our heavenly Father, so will a marriage die when a couple refuses to communicate. Ephesians 4:29-30 reveals that the purpose of communication is to edify, not corrupt. The Holy Spirit is grieved when we are not ministers of grace.

The varied assignments for this session cover communication extensively—nonverbal communication, communication guidelines, effective communication, scenario communication.

Our communication goals include the following: to share with one another freely; to be lovingly honest about what we think and feel; to understand each other; to listen respectfully and respond appropriately; to be able to disagree and discuss our disagreements without becoming hurt or attacking one another; and to have conversation that is beneficial and uplifting.

Norm Wright, in his book *Training Christians to Counsel*, states that communication is made up of the following components:

    7% words (content)

    38% attitude (tone of voice)

    55% body language

It will be vital for you to emphasize the importance of healthy communication. As you and the couple work together, you will have the opportunity to refer to unhealthy methods of communication, as well as the tone of voice and body language employed by the counselees.

James 4:1-2 informs us that conflicts come from wanting something but not getting it. In order to help the couple work through possible communication difficulties, the following synopsis for conflict resolution should be helpful.

A. Decision-making is a large part of the conflict resolution process.

Ask: Who made the decisions in their families of origin?
Who will exert more influence in decision-making in this new family?
Who will be ultimately responsible for decisions made?
How has the couple been making decisions independently?
How have they been making decisions during their engagement period?
How have they escaped decision-making in the past?

B. Take practical steps to resolve conflict. (Remember, when conflict comes, you tend to focus on yourself.)

1. Don't demand; listen (Proverbs 18:13).
2. Select the right time and place (Proverbs 15:23).
3. Define the problem area.
4. Define the areas of agreement and disagreement.
5. Identify your contribution to the problem—accept some responsibility.
6. Identify the behaviors you need to change.
7. Listen to the feelings of the other person. (Feelings do not need to be factual; however, you can agree that your spouse is "feeling" this way.)
8. Find out what the Word of God says about the problem area.
9. Pray together and agree on necessary changes.

Covering the following verses will be helpful: Proverbs 13:18; 23:12; 25:12; 28:13; Philippians 3:13.

Finances

Premarital Session Four

Conflicting ideas about finances often cause marital dysfunction. In many of the divorces filed each year in our country, complaints often involve finances.

God gives clear guidelines and principles for handling finances in His Word. Truth about finances can be found in Scripture.

Also included in this session are assignments which will clarify personal views about finances, work sheets concerned with cost estimation and a budget profile. Take time to cover the budget profile with the couple. Be sensitive to any potential problems in the financial area. (It is recommended that you as counselors familiarize yourself with this budget profile by inserting your personal financial figures.)

In Session Four, you will want to discuss financial expectations. For example, a couple may expect to purchase a new home within the first year of marriage; they may need to buy a second car or decide to replace one of their present vehicles with a newer one; they may unconsciously expect to be at the financial level of their parents or another couple whom they admire before that can be a reality. It will be important for you as counselors to confront these financial issues candidly.

As mentors, you have the opportunity to guide this couple toward trusting God for their finances rather than trusting credit cards, loans or family members. Prayerfully consider sharing Luke 12:22-31 with this couple. God is their Source.

Finally, teaching this couple to love God more than money is a basic foundation to their life together. Having a relationship with God and with others is more important than any *thing*. First Timothy 6:1-12 would be appropriate to close Session Four with.

Sexual Relations

Premarital Session Five

God is the creator of sex. He originated lovemaking between married partners. Sex is "a beautiful and intimate relationship shared uniquely by a husband and wife," as stated by Tim and Beverly LaHaye in their book *The Act of Marriage*.

In His Word, God has given information and directions concerning sexual relations. He doesn't consider sex an embarrassing topic. He addresses marriage in a discreet and wholesome way. As counselors, we need to follow God's lead. We need to be sources of helpful and practical information. Many couples go into marriage unprepared, naive and sadly misinformed about sexuality and sexual relations. Many Christian marriages are lacking vitality and are less than God's best, leaving unfulfilled partners to continue without hope of change.

Homework exercises found in this session will open up discussion on attitudes and beliefs about sex, scriptural references to sex in marriage and will include matching definitions of sexual terms, identification of male and female anatomy and true/false statements regarding areas of sexuality. (Answers to these final three exercises are found in Appendix E.) Assess the couple's abilities to express themselves about sex: Are they embarrassed, fearful, disgusted, naive, or do they use inappropriate terminology? As counselors, it is imperative that you use correct sexual terminology and to not be embarrassed by these terms. Pre- and postmarital counselors must be comfortable discussing the topic of sex and entertaining any questions that the counselee couple may have. Use Scripture to address any misguided attitudes. Offer practical advice for the honeymoon (see Appendix D). Reassure the couple that you will be available for counsel in the postmarital relationship.

Ceremony Planning

Premarital Session Six

The exercises in this section are extremely important for the premarital counselors, as well as the minister who will perform the ceremony. If you have served a couple through premarital counseling, but you are not going to perform the marriage ceremony, you will need to give your input and assessment to the minister. If your assessment of this couple is that they are not prepared for marriage or if you believe they are premature in their call together, then they must be lovingly advised.

Take special note of the exercise "Saying I Do." Your emphasis should be on the spiritual union that occurs during a marriage ceremony. Please familiarize yourself with these seven areas. You may encourage the couple to discuss some of the points with their parents. After the sample ceremony, take a realistic look at the honeymoon and ask the couple some candid questions. The honeymoon is an important part of the wedding planning. Take time to walk the couple through their expectations of this event.

The final exercise in this chapter is a study on "submission," a very misunderstood topic in the church today. It is our belief that this study is simple, clear, theologically sound and very helpful in comprehending the topic. As counselors, be clear on the biblical definition and scriptural references to submission. Be prepared to give examples from your mission together as premarital counselors and practically how submission has developed in your relationship. (Suggestion: Share with the couple how giving pre- and postmarital training is a cooperative mission, one which gives you the opportunity to submit to one another.)

It is very important that the couple enjoy each aspect of the planning—from choosing invitations, gowns and flowers to writing their vows and making arrangements for the honeymoon. Caution the couple not to allow themselves to become anxious or frustrated with details. This is a one-time experience, and they will be grateful for happy memories.

Counselor's Guide to

Postmarital Sessions

Called Together
Postmarital Course Overview

Introduction to the Postmarital Course

A. Goals of Postmarital Training:

1. To reinforce premarital instruction and implementation of that information
2. To provide an assessment of the positive growth within this new marriage
3. To focus on specific or potential problem areas within this marriage

B. Sub-goals of Postmarital Training:

1. To aid the couple in evaluating their present relationship
2. To provide helpful dialogue between the newly married couple and the postmarital counselors
3. To aid the couple in the further development of spiritual skills, communication skills, financial skills and sexual skills

C. Objectives of Postmarital Training will be met:

1. By attending at least two postmarital sessions
2. By readministering a relationship profile
3. By reviewing appropriate premarital information
4. By modeling/dialoguing aspects of the marriage relationship with the couple and counselors
5. By completing reading and writing assignments
6. By participating in prayer and Bible study

Before Postmarital Session One

A general guideline for postmarital education would be to meet with the couple at three months and nine months after the wedding. The postmarital course is designed with a minimum of two sessions in mind. You may meet with this couple as often as necessary. Note that the areas of review in this guide are broken down into two sessions. Discuss "Spiritual Overview" and "Communication Overview" at the three-month session. "Financial Overview" and "Sexual Overview" can be reviewed at the nine-month session.

It is assumed that you were the couple's premarital counselors. If you did not perform the premarital counseling, then have a get-acquainted session. In this meeting you will need to gather as much background information as possible. You could use your *Called Together* manual as an outline for questioning.

Require the couple to turn in their *Called Together* three-month postmarital assignments before the scheduled session. You will also want them to bring their relationship profiles. If you are certified to administer a profile, you will want to readminister it to the couple and note any personality/behavior differences in their graphs. It is extremely profitable to profile the couple during the postmarital training.

We recommend the books *If Only He Knew*, by Gary Smalley, and *The Man in Your Life,* by Norm Wright, be given to the husband and wife, respectively, at the first postmarital session and completed by the last session.

The second set of exercises are to be completed and turned in to you before the nine-month session. This will give you time to review the couple's responses and make note of specific areas of discussion.

Build upon the relationship that you established during the premarital course now in the more realistic postmarital counseling sessions. Always keep in mind that counseling couples toward a Christ-centered marriage will influence their children and generations to come. Your example, warmth, love, confrontation, empathy and understanding translate into an act "to prepare God's people for works of service" (Ephesians 4:12). There is no greater ministry than serving and building the Christian family!

Areas of Review for Postmarital Session One

A. Spiritual Overview:

1. Where is the couple in their relationship with Jesus Christ? Is this couple attending a church as a family, involved in daily family devotions, involved in daily individual devotions, praying with one another, tithing and giving to others?

2. What are their spiritual goals (for example, being involved in short-term missions or long-term missions, leading a home fellowship group, ministering to others)?

3. What will help to make this couple spiritually successful? Please cover the following verses with the couple.

   a. Our sufficiency is in Christ: 2 Corinthians 3:5-6—"Not that we are competent in ourselves to claim anything for ourselves, but our competence comes from God. He has made us competent as ministers of a new covenant—not of the letter but of the Spirit; for the letter kills, but the Spirit gives life."

   b. Be effective and productive Christians: 2 Peter 1:5-9—"For this very reason, make every effort to add to your faith goodness; and to goodness, knowledge; and to knowledge, self-control; and to self-control, perseverance; and to perseverance, godliness; and to godliness, brother kindness; and to brotherly kindness, love. For if you possess these qualities in increasing measure, they will keep you from being ineffective and unproductive in your knowledge of our Lord Jesus Christ. But if anyone does not have them, he is nearsighted and blind, and has forgotten that he has been cleansed from his past sins."

   Matthew 6:21—"For where your treasure is, there your heart will be also."

   c. We need not fear; He holds the future: 1 John 4:18—"There is no fear in love. But perfect love drives out fear, because fear has to do with punishment. The one who fears is not made perfect in love."

Philippians 3:13; 4:6—"Brothers, I do not consider myself yet to have taken hold of it. But one thing I do: Forgetting what is behind and straining toward what is ahead. . . . Do not be anxious about anything, but in everything, by prayer and petition, with thanksgiving, present your requests to God."

d. Trust and know God: Proverbs 3:5-6—"Trust in the LORD with all your heart and lean not on your own understanding; in all your ways acknowledge him, and he will make your paths straight."

Mark 9:23—"Everything is possible for him who believes."
Jeremiah 32:27—" 'I am the LORD, the God of all mankind. Is anything too hard for me?' "
Jeremiah 9:23-24—"This is what the LORD says: 'Let not the wise man boast of his wisdom or the strong man boast of his strength or the rich man boast of his riches, but let him who boasts boast about this: that he understands and knows me, that I am the LORD, who exercises kindness, justice and righteousness on earth, for in these I delight,' declares the LORD."

e. Be a doer: James 1:22-23—"Do not merely listen to the word, and so deceive yourselves. Do what it says. Anyone who listens to the word but does not do what it says is like a man who looks at his face in the mirror. . . ."

B. Communication Overview:

1. Turn to pages 16-17 of the *Called Together* manual. How has the couple dealt with the expectations about which they previously wrote? Are there new areas of expectation?
2. Review the practical steps to resolve conflict found at the end of the Communication section of the counselor's guide along with James 4:1-2. Review Norm Wright's analysis of communication. Ask the couple to share how they have been resolving conflicts.

3. What has the couple discovered about nonverbal communication? Are there any ways in which a spouse has experienced negative nonverbal communication? Discuss this.
4. Review Communication Guidelines on page 33.
5. Review appropriate Do You Discuss questions found on page 38. (For example, is the couple showing their feelings and attitudes, differences and hurts without anger and criticism?)
6. Assignment: Reread chapter 11, "The Secret of Staying in Love" (especially for newlyweds), in the book *Love Life for Every Married Couple* by Dr. Ed Wheat.

Note: Are you accountable in the above areas? Be certain that your marriage is a Christ-centered, positive example to the couple you are counseling.

Areas of Review for Session Two

C. Financial Overview:

1. Review Personal Financial Views (page 44). How have the couple's premarital views changed? Cover again all fifteen questions.
2. Take the couple through a review of the Scriptures found on page 47. Are they walking in accordance with God's Word in the financial realm?
3. Is the couple using the Personal Finances Budget Sheet found on page 49 or are they keeping records with a different tool? Ask the couple to complete a new budget sheet. They can use the line item instructions found on page 123 of the *Called Together* postmarital material.
4. Thoroughly review their financial status. Are they tithing? Do they have concrete places in which to invest for their future (e.g., IRA, retirement, real estate)? Do they live in a high rent area? Is their rent within their budget? Carefully look over the utilities. How much is their monthly telephone bill? Are long distance calls within reason? Has the couple incurred new debt? Is a vehicle payment restricting them financially? Are they spending money for date nights? Is the couple overinsured/underinsured? Is the couple saving for annual or semi-annual bills? Are their present bills current?
5. Question whether or not this couple is walking in financial agreement. Are they accountable to one another in their spending? Do they give one another an allowance? If there is a financial need, are they willing to trust God to see that need met?
6. Can this couple live on the husband's salary or are they depending upon the wife's income as well? Discuss this thoroughly along with their financial goals. Ask the couple how their goals may change when children arrive.
7. Pray for God's blessing on their finances. Share with them that God is their provider. The ultimate source is not their job, the bank, the church or their parents.

Note: Keep in mind that as an older, wiser couple, you can help hold this younger couple accountable with their finances, if they wish. A review of the financial status and financial goals will indicate how realistic this couple is in relation to their income and expenditures.

D. Sexual Overview:

1. Go over appropriate "Questions for Discussion" found on pages 57-58 (questions 2, 4, 5, 6 and 11).
2. What attitudes or beliefs about sex have surfaced since the wedding night? (See page 59 as a guideline.)
3. What sexual complications has the couple encountered? Are they both experiencing orgasm? Are they free to communicate their sexual needs with one another?
4. Thoroughly review "A Creative Plan" found on pages 63-65. (Note: Encourage the couple to listen to Dr. Ed Wheat's *Sex Techniques* tapes. This series of two 90-minute cassettes focuses specifically upon the area of physical unity within marriage.)
5. Does the couple have any questions concerning birth control? See Appendix C (pg. 213-215). Have their plans for having children changed now that they are married?
6. A second series of two 90-minute cassette tapes by Dr. Ed Wheat is also recommended. This series, entitled "Love Life," offers personal counsel and practical insights on the principles of building love within the marriage.

Assignment: Reread chapters 6, 11, 13 in Dr. Ed Wheat's book *Love Life for Every Married Couple*.

Note: Be sure to remind the couple to utilize Tim and Beverly LaHaye's book *The Act of Marriage* as a helpful reference.

For seminar or workshop presentations contact:
Steve and Mary Prokopchak
1924 West Main Street
Ephrata, PA 17522
Telephone: 717-738-3751